A DELICATE ART

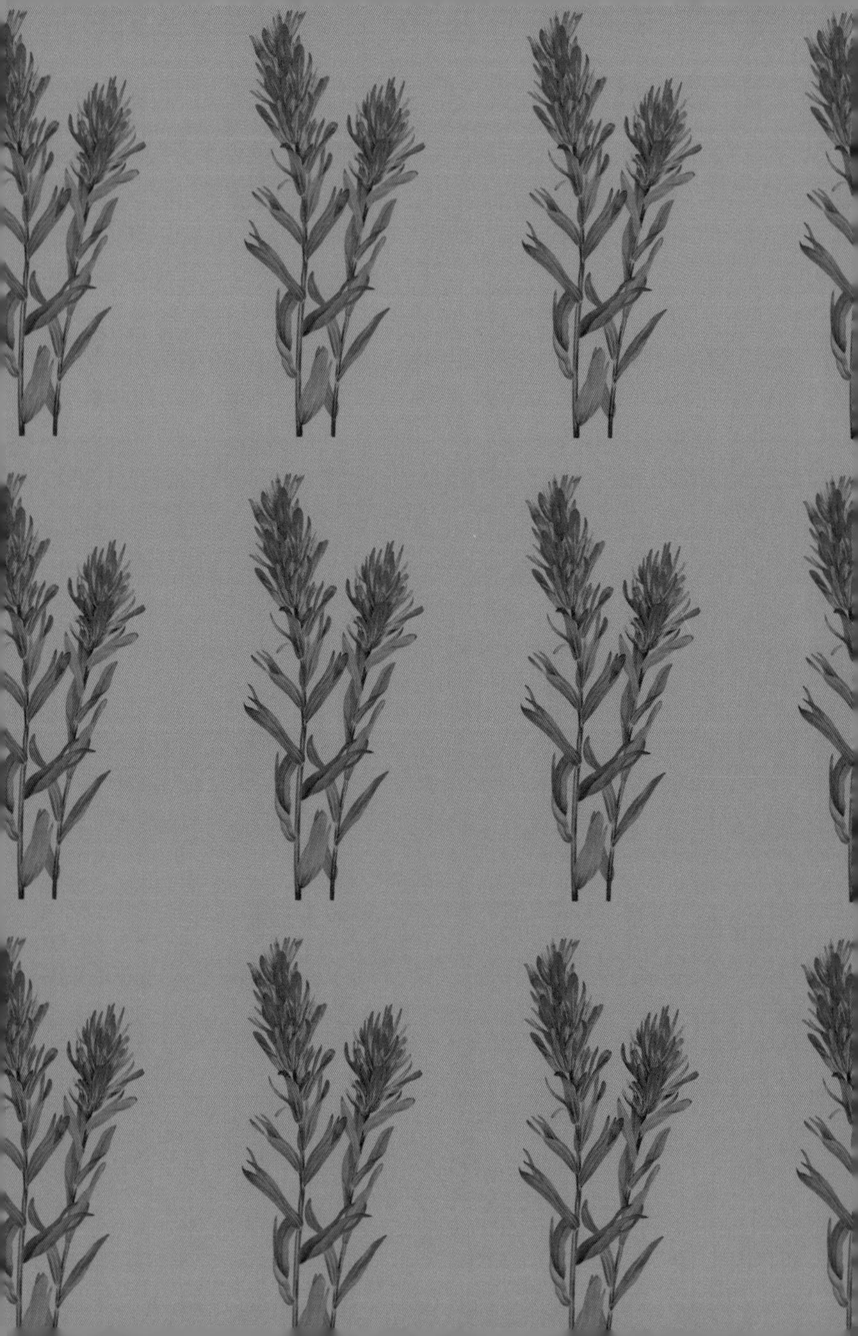

A *Delicate* Art

Artists, Wildflowers and Native Plants of the West

Mary-Beth Laviolette

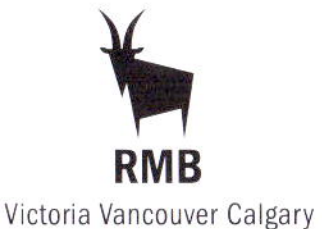

RMB
Victoria Vancouver Calgary

Rocky Mountain Books
www.rmbooks.com

Library and Archives Canada Cataloguing in Publication

Laviolette, Mary-Beth
A delicate art : artists, wildflowers and native plants of the West / Mary-Beth Laviolette.

Includes bibliographical references and index.

ISBN 978-1-927330-05-0

1. Wild flowers in art—Alberta—History.
2. Wild flowers—Rocky Mountains, Canadian (B.C. and Alta.)—Pictorial works.
3. Endemic plants—Rocky Mountains, Canadian (B.C. and Alta.)—Pictorial works.
4. Botanical illustration—Rocky Mountains, Canadian (B.C. and Alta.).
5. Painters—Alberta—Biography.
6. Painting, Canadian—20th century.
7. Nature photography—Rocky Mountains, Canadian (B.C. and Alta.).
8. Photographers—Alberta—Biography. I. Title.

N7680.L39 2012 704.9'4343 C2011-908608-5

Printed in Canada

Rocky Mountain Books acknowledges the financial support for its publishing program from the Government of Canada through the Canada Book Fund (CBF) and the Canada Council for the Arts, and from the province of British Columbia through the British Columbia Arts Council and the Book Publishing Tax Credit.

Canadian Heritage Patrimoine canadien

Canada Council for the Arts Conseil des Arts du Canada

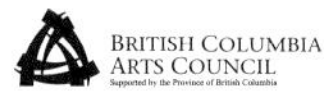

This book was produced using FSC®-certified, acid-free paper, processed chlorine free and printed with vegetable-based inks.

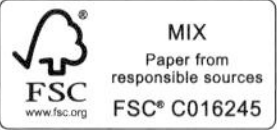

In honour of their floral enthusiasms,
from whom I have learned so much:
Cheri Sydor, Laura Kenwood,
Patricia Ainslie, and my
mother, Irene Laviolette.

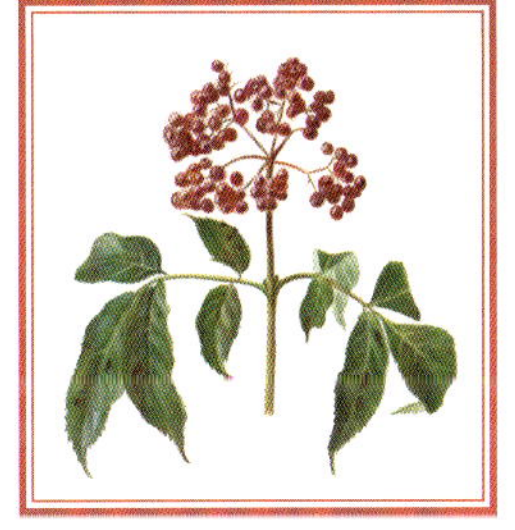

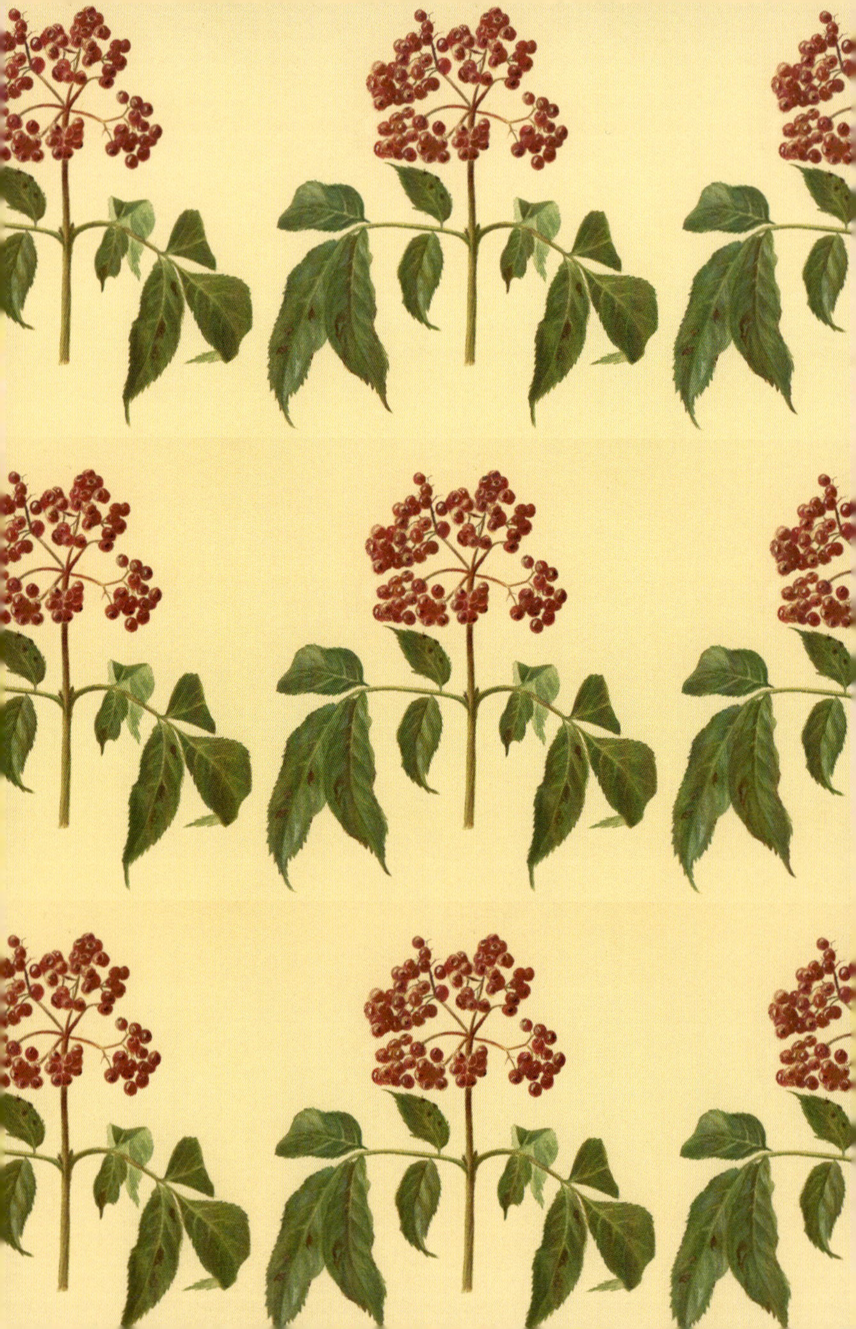

Contents

Acknowledgements 9

Introduction 12

Mary Schäffer Warren 21

Mary Vaux Walcott 39

William Copeland McCalla 59

Annora Brown 79

Robert Sinclair 103

Carole Harmon 121

Notes 139

Sources and further reading 145

List of Artworks 150

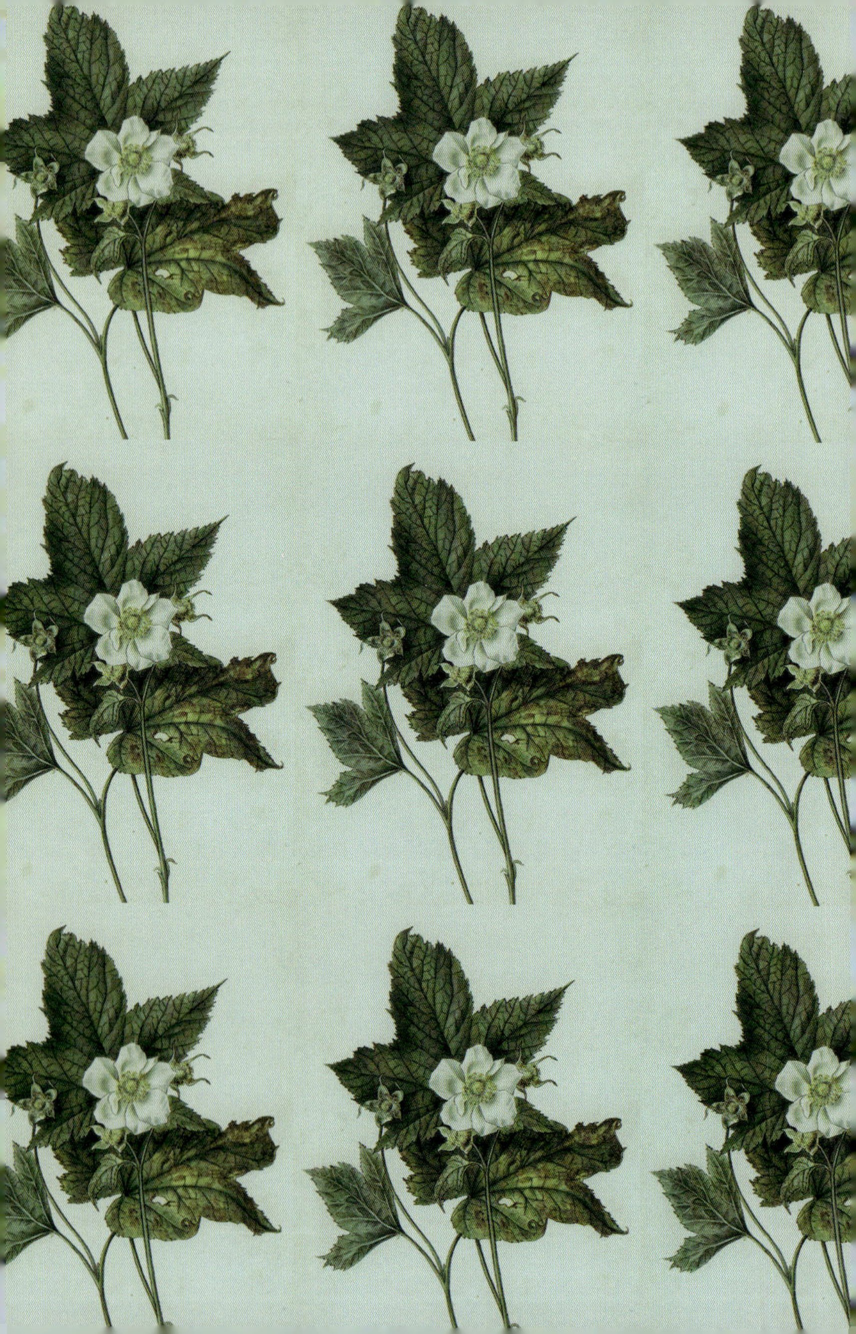

Acknowledgements

I first want to acknowledge the generous help I received from friends who gave their time and energies in assisting with the preparation of this book. My thanks to Linda Diener, who spent many hours checking and matching the correct Latin names with the common names of plants featured. To Laura Kenwood, who kindly read the entire manuscript as it was being written and who offered her opinions and suggestions. Ditto for Patricia Alderson, whose expertise on Annora Brown was an invaluable contribution as well. And finally, thanks to Michele Corbeil, who assembled the bibliography for the book.

Recognition must also be given to artists Robert Sinclair and Carole Harmon, who agreed to allow their artwork and personal stories to be included, in effect giving readers an opportunity to see how the subject of wildflowers continues to inspire new interpretations. Carole must also be thanked for introducing me to the marvellous work of William Copeland McCalla. Thanks also to curator Dean Tatam Reeves of The Esplanade (Medicine Hat, Alta.), who organized a recent travelling exhibition of McCalla's work. Once I was hooked, archivist Marlena Wyman at the Provincial Archives of Alberta provided invaluable assistance. A nod of recognition must also go to the helpful McCalla family, including Donna L. Clandfield and Dennis McCalla.

The Whyte Museum of the Canadian Rockies in Banff houses fine examples of the watercolours and photography of Mary Schäffer and Mary Vaux Walcott, who died on the eve of the Second World War. The museum is a remarkable cultural resource and I would like to express my gratitude to the Whyte's Michale Lang, Deserae Komar and Craig Richards, as well as, at the Whyte Library & Archives, Lena Goon and Elizabeth Kundert-Cameron for their cooperation. In addition, I would like to thank Schäffer biographer Janice Sanford Beck; Professor Henry Vaux; and Sarah Stauderman, Smithsonian Institution Archives for their time and information.

Annora Brown's artwork was assembled from the collections of Arctos & Bird, Banff (Peter Poole and Susan Wanamaker); The Eleanor Luxton Foundation, Banff (Ralphine Locke); and the Alberta Foundation for the Arts (Gail Lint and Neil Lazaruk). Patricia Alderson assisted in contacting the Brown estate for permission to reproduce the artist′s watercolours. Thank you to all.

Finally, a great deal of appreciation goes to Susan Sax

and Tom Willock of Willock & Sax Gallery, Banff, for their careful work in creating digital images of Annora Brown and Robert Sinclair artworks for publication. Dan Hudson played a similar role with other images.

And last but not least, a hug for husband Douglas MacLean, whose knowledge about Annora Brown paintings and Canadian art in general has created such a loving bond between us.

Mary-Beth Laviolette
Canmore, Alberta
February 2012

INTRODUCTION

To see a world in a grain of sand
and a heaven in a wild flower

—WILLIAM BLAKE,
Auguries of Innocence (1803)

The visionary poet and artist William Blake had it right. There *is* a heaven in a wildflower. And I am sure that what is most striking about even the tiniest bloom is the sheer perfection and beauty of it all. Metaphorically too, much can be read into these denizens of the wild. Take the shooting star, with its comet-like streaming petals, or the hardy harebell, with its nodding, bell-shaped flowers on hair-like stems. Despite the harebell's resilience, is it still not the essence of fragility? Of course, from a scientific standpoint, it's all about reproduction and the creation of seeds, but nonetheless be amazed (and humbled) by what springs forth in colour, shape, size and, most of all, adaptation.

I once read that gardening is an art shaped by the

gardener. In the case of the wildflower, it's nature's job. But her actions can be capricious and inexplicable. Where the gardener might seek to impose some kind of order, nature will do no such thing. At least, not in the way we humans might think of order. Wildflowers can carpet the landscape in a tangled web of vibrant growth, or appear only reluctantly, in the scantiest of numbers. Some species can also defy the odds and flourish in the most hostile of conditions, whether natural or man-made.

But before going any further, I would like to point out that *A Delicate Art* is not a guidebook about wildflowers and how they thrive. Instead, from my own happy memories of such floral encounters, I have gathered together a selection of artwork and the fascinating stories of six artists who have made a serious study of this remarkable subject. What these artists have in common is the fact that they have covered some of the same ground as I have, from the Northern Rockies near Jasper all the way south to Waterton Lakes National Park and from the Kootenays of southern British Columbia to the towering Selkirks of Rogers Pass and Revelstoke. To the east of the mountains too, there are the unique landscapes of southern Alberta: the grasslands of the ranch country, the coulees and badlands, and, on the Alberta–Saskatchewan boundary, the incomparable Cypress Hills.

A Delicate Art spans more than a hundred years, beginning with the Victorian-bred Mary Schäffer and closing with Carole Harmon, born after the Second World War. In between, there is Schäffer's friend Mary Vaux Walcott; the pioneer botanist and teacher William Copeland McCalla, who likely didn't consider himself an artist; the early Alberta painter and raconteur Annora Brown; and the superb watercolourist Robert Sinclair. Of these six hunters of flora, four are also authors, each of them having contributed a book on native plants, including the seminal *North American Wildflowers*, by Mary Vaux Walcott.

So, is *A Delicate Art* a book about botanical art? Yes and no. Both Marys – Schäffer and Vaux – certainly painted with an informed eye on the long tradition of botanical illustration. With an emphasis on detailed observation and a concern for scientifically correct rendering, botanical art is sometimes viewed as a minor form concerned only with creating exact copies. But in a beautiful exhibition catalogue titled *A New Flowering: 1000 Years of Botanical Art*, a more nuanced understanding of the subject is underlined by Professor Lucia Tongiorgi Tomasi: "Every botanical artist aspires to capture the truth, yet the same plant portrayed by different hands will always appear new to our eyes because it is interpreted with a different sensibility linked to a different culture."[1]

What the two Marys expressed in watercolour is certainly in step with the botanical illustration of their time. What Annora Brown, Robert Sinclair and Carole Harmon have created, though, is rooted in something else: the modern art tradition. They are, in fact, artists of a different calling, where the stress is on personal expression and experimentation. Wildflowers and other native perennials are treated with respect but with the idea of allowing the plant to thrive in different conditions. Those conditions are linked to the poetic, the metaphorical, the interpretative, as well as the sheer aesthetics of representing such an engaging subject.

As for William Copeland McCalla, because of his strong connections to the academic study of botany, he belongs with the two Marys. But, in common with those two earlier floraphiliacs, his photographs and lantern slides were made with a broader public in mind, especially the schoolteachers McCalla instructed. In an era of widening public education and with the aid of other forms of public presentation such as photographs and projecting slides in a darkened room, the passionate work of these three early pioneers was intended for the specialist and the layperson alike.

The choice of watercolours, photo collages and hand-painted lantern slides reproduced in *A Delicate Art* are, of course, only a very small selection of the work made by these six artists. My intention is to show how varied and inventive the treatment of wildflowers and other native plants can be. As with other subjects in art, flowers are a source of inspiration and an invitation to the artist to meld their chosen medium and skill with their observant eye. Wildflowers, flowering shrubs and their berries, and in one case the cones of a tree (western larch), comprise the selection of flora represented in this book.

Some, like the western wood lily, appear here more than once, though portrayed differently each time, since no two interpretations are alike. Some can found growing almost anywhere, such as the prickly rose (*Rosa acicularis*), which became Alberta's floral emblem in 1930 after it was voted on by the province's schoolchildren. Hence the oft-repeated phrase about Alberta being "Wild Rose Country." On the other side of the coin, a few of the plants depicted here are quite rare. For instance, I have yet to see the many-flowered Indian pipe (*Monotropa hypopitys*), with its urn-shaped flowers and scale-like leaves, which William Copeland McCalla was fortunate to find in a rich coniferous forest.

From McCalla's large oeuvre I have also chosen his

picture of the common dandelion (*Taraxacum officinale*), an invasive species that some may not consider suitable for inclusion in a book such as this. Nevertheless, McCalla's treatment of this successful immigrant is simply outstanding and transcends the simple inventorying of nature. I also was surprised to read in Annora Brown's wildflower book how recent an arrival this plant actually is. Brown recounts that, according to local lore, "the [common dandelion] was first brought to this continent by the Hudson's Bay Company traders at Fort Churchill, who needed it to balance a diet consisting too largely of meat."[2]

Finally, this introduction to *A Delicate Art* cannot close without mention of how wildflowers and native plants are attracting more public interest these days. In this part of Canada it's not unusual to come across news about the cultivation of wild species in places where even urban dwellers can appreciate this gift from nature. In Lethbridge, for instance, the Centennial Native Prairie Plant Garden, recently established by volunteers from the Lethbridge & District Horticultural Society, is located right at the entrance of the Galt Museum, itself impressively sited on the shoulder of an eroded coulee high above the Oldman River. Similar, but older in pedigree and serving as a more northerly oasis for plant life, is the Devonian Botanical Garden, located on the outskirts of Edmonton. The facility has acres of display gardens, including a Native People's Garden showcasing trees, shrubs and herbaceous plants used by the first people of Alberta.

Along this theme, there is also the Banff Centre's Butterfly Garden, a collection of butterfly-attracting subalpine species planted by the late Mike MacDonald. MacDonald was an artist of mixed aboriginal and European ancestry who, after hearing from a native elder that these colourful insects represented the spirits of deceased medicine people, planted some twenty butterfly gardens across the country to show people the significant role native plants play in the lives of the First Nations. When you are not feeling well, goes the belief, follow a butterfly and it will lead you to a medicinal plant.

Of course, outside of these cultivated sanctuaries, there are the hundreds – no, *thousands* – of hiking boots and running shoes put to the trail every spring, summer and fall. Nothing replaces the amazement some feel when encountering a field full of wildflowers up high at Lake O'Hara or in Banff's Sunshine Meadows. Both are places where ski tracks melt away to reveal treasures of the alpine soil. Even earlier in the season are the pleasures found at a lower altitude such as in Waterton Lakes National Park, where in mid-June there is a popular wildflower festival.

Every attempt has been made to match the correct Latin name with the common name(s) of these plants. I was told by Joyce Gould, a botanist for Alberta parks, that as vascular flora these species will all find their rightful place in a new three-volume work being prepared to reflect changes in taxonomy and new discoveries, particularly in the boreal forest. So, with the advent of this new work covering approximately 1,700 species – including trees and shrubs – and to readers of the many new guidebooks available to both the dedicated and the just curious, I offer these stories and artworks of six individuals who have brought pencils, brushes and cameras to this delightful subject.

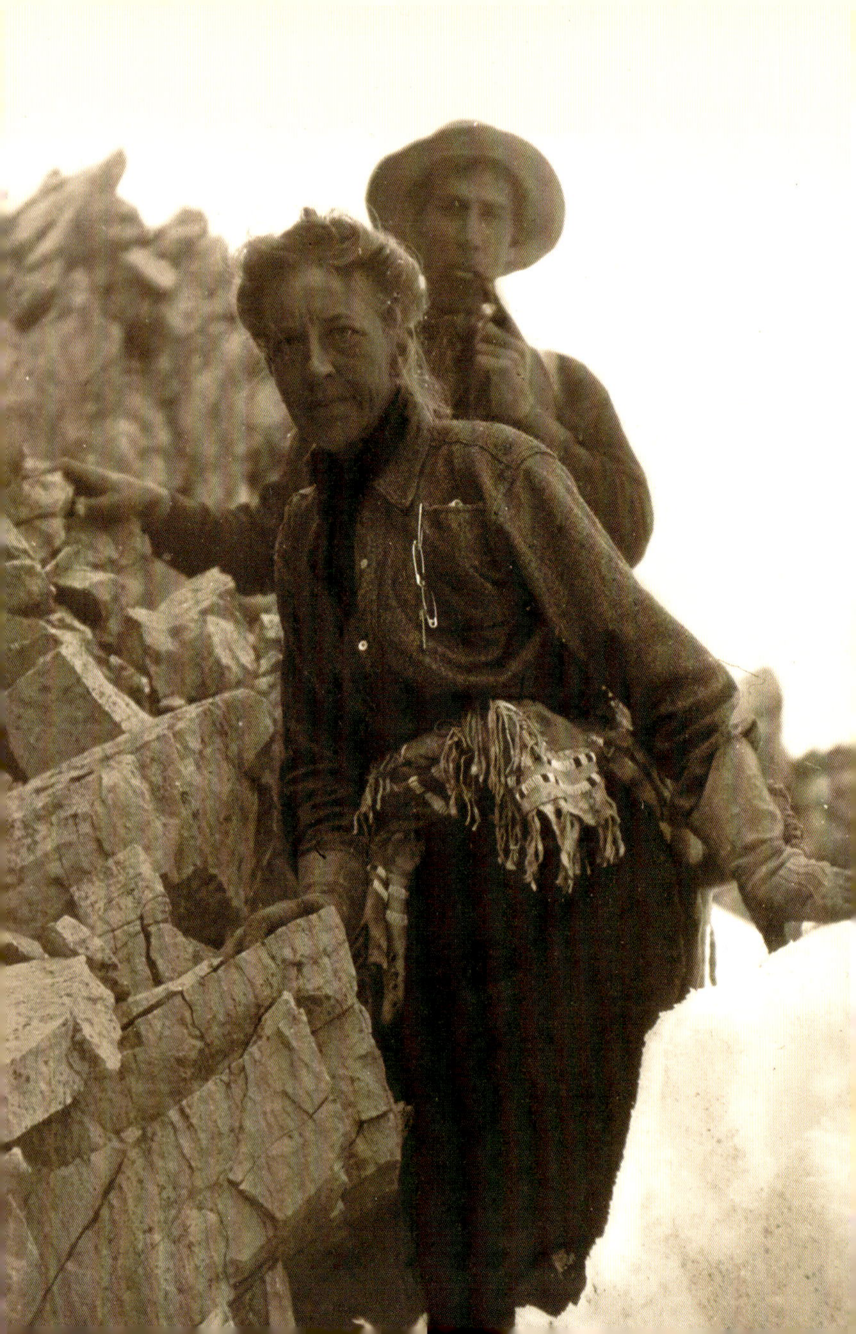

1

Mary Schäffer Warren
(1861–1939)

Mary Schäffer Warren had a particular "garden" in mind when she told her hometown audience in Philadelphia about a place where "for hundreds of miles stretches this garden of mine, clasped in the snowy embrace of the great white Rockies":

> No gardener tends my treasures, only the spring sunshine, which coaxes them forth, the summer rains which wash their dainty faces, and the deep, deep blankets of snow which cover the seeds, the bulbs and roots, and cuddles them all close to warm Mother Earth's breast.[3]

Part of a public talk given by Schäffer in 1909, "My Garden" is an enthusiastic piece of prose – part travelogue, part garden tour – that begins in Banff and finishes several hundred kilometres north at Maligne Lake, near Jasper. Along the way, by horse and on foot, Mary will encounter nearly two-dozen species on her "march of flowers." One is the lemon-coloured snow lily or, as it is more commonly known today, the glacier lily. Often bursting forth just as the snow recedes, this early-season food for bears triggered strong emotions in this well-bred Victorian "lady":

> Sinking down on a mossy bed, I touched, caressed, revelled in their odor, buried my face in their own bright petals, and half-hidden among them, lay and watched the butterflies, dragon flies and bees, the little robbers stealing the honey from my great golden preserve.[4]

As a painter, accomplished photographer, writer and "hunter" of flora, Schäffer had, for close to two decades, spent many summers in the western mountains. Already noted as a photographer and watercolour illustrator for her work with botanist Stewardson Brown on their 1907 book *Alpine Flora of the Canadian Rocky Mountains*, by the time Schäffer penned "My Garden" a few years later, she was increasingly renowned as an adventurer and explorer. The latter reputation became definitively established when Mary located Maligne Lake, one of the great scenic icons of the Canadian Rockies. This unusual piece of trail-blazing was achieved in 1908 in the company of

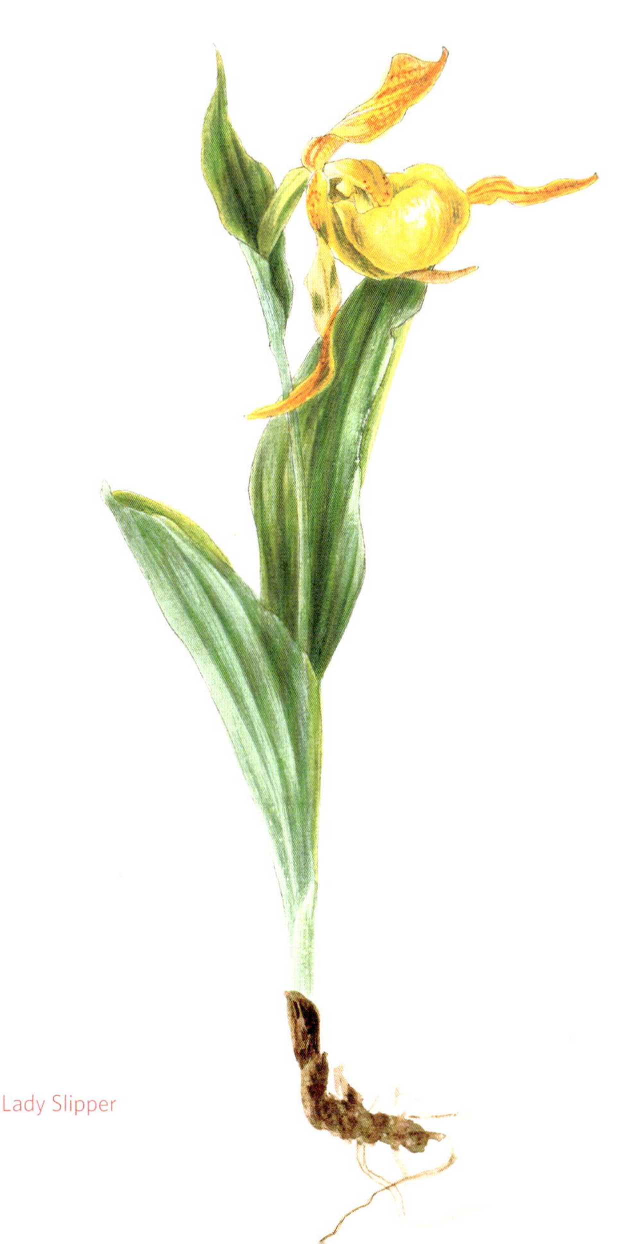

Lady Slipper

her close friend, geology teacher Mollie Adams of New York, Stewardson Brown of Philadelphia and their three able guides from Banff, Billy Warren, Reggie Holmes and Sid Unwin with his dog, Mr. Muggins.

A rough map supplied by a Stoney Nakoda, Samson Beaver, had provided some guidance for finding a route to the mysterious lake. Much to her credit, Mary Schäffer never claimed her group were the first people to stand on the gravel shoreline of Chaba Imne, as the Stoneys called the lake. The title of her follow-up book, the very popular *Old Indian Trails of the Canadian Rockies*, reaffirmed her debt to those earlier travellers, including Beaver, who had seen the impressive lake when he was a young boy. Schäffer's now-classic 1911 book is an engaging memoir of her two-summer exploration through the daunting backcountry of Banff and Jasper. As a review in the *New York Times* put it, "[I]t is difficult to decide just what impresses us most: the excellence of the writing, the picturesqueness of the country described, or the personality of the author herself."[5]

If I had to choose, I would put the emphasis on Schäffer's personality: determined and willing no matter what the social codes of her day were. Turning heads too was her outdoor attire, which by then consisted of a shortened riding skirt, hobnail boots and a distinctive Indian buckskin jacket. Beautifully crafted by a Jasper pioneer

Métis, Suzette Chalifoux Swift, this jacket is later noted in the travel writings of the English poet and author Rudyard Kipling. On a trip in the Banff area, the famous British imperialist passes Schäffer on a trail. Seated in his carriage, Kipling mistakes her for a native woman with her bare head, tanned face and signature beaded jacket. She is also, as Kipling records it, "riding straddle"[6] on her horse, something no true lady would ever do!

Alpine Flora of the Canadian Rockies contains some of the earliest published examples of botanical art by Schäffer, with over thirty full-page coloured plates of watercolours and nearly a hundred black & white photographs. Despite this achievement, it was not the first time her work had been seen publicly. In 1900, at a Paris exhibition of photography by American women, eight of her silver prints were displayed, all of them photographs of flowers with the exception of a picture of Mount Sir Donald at Rogers Pass. Her beautiful hand-coloured lantern slides* were also exhibited internationally and in 1896 earned her a lifetime membership in the Academy of Natural Sciences of Philadelphia.

Complementing these skills with camera and

* Developed from the negative, the 3¼" x 4" glass lantern slide was projected on a wall or screen so that photographic images could be viewed by a larger audience, a precursor of the smaller 35mm slides used later in the 20th century. For more on this early photographic technology and Mary Schäffer's artistically accomplished use of it, see, for example, Michale Lang's *An Adventurous Woman Abroad: The Selected Lantern Slides of Mary T.S. Schäffer* (Calgary: Rocky Mountain Books, 2011).

brush was Mary's adept handling of the flower press, a 400-year-old device designed to allow maximum airflow as the plant or flower is pressed dry. In the Victorian era, pressed flower art was very fashionable among women of Schäffer's social standing, though in her case the precious specimens were pressed and dried daily for examination by her husband, Dr. Charles Schäffer, a medical doctor and plant lover whom she had married in 1889.

Charles Schäffer, like his much younger wife, was a Quaker and a Philadelphian who loved spending summers in the high alpine. On their travels together, he came to the conclusion that, apart from earlier collecting by the Palliser Expedition's remarkable Eugène Bourgeau* and later by John Macoun,** an important contribution to science could be made with an illustrated botanical guide covering the largely unknown territory between Banff and Rogers Pass.

* Eugène Bourgeau (1813–1877), who named Lac des Arcs and Grotto Mountain near Canmore, Alberta, was amazed by the many new species he found in the Rockies in 1858. Some of the specimens he collected may still be seen at the Royal Botanical Gardens at Kew, a centre of plant science, conservation and botanical illustration near London, England.

** John Macoun (1831–1920) also collected mountain plants, as well as butterflies, in the Canmore area before proceeding to Banff and other station stops along the way on the newly built CPR in 1885. His 20-year work, the *Catalogue of Canadian Plants*, earned him the sobriquet "The Father of Canadian Botany."

The field of natural history in the 18th and 19th centuries is especially rich with the detailed observations and cataloguing of flora and fauna by amateurs. People did this work for the love of it, as Charles and Mary did, and they were fortunate to live in an era when the dedicated amateur could make a difference *and* be taken seriously by the more formally trained. Though Charles was already a member of the Academy of Natural Sciences of Philadelphia, he apparently did not realize, when he and Mary first embarked on their dream project in the Rockies, that in addition to the delicate ritual of pressing and drying plants, Mary had a real talent for drawing and painting them as well, which could be incorporated into their joint upcoming book.

In fact, during Mary's upbringing, as Mary Townsend Sharpless, daughter of a well-off Quaker family in Philadelphia, the study of nature and art had gone hand-in hand. Her father, Alfred, was, like Charles, another thoroughly engaged "amateur," and from him Mary received serious exposure to the fruits of "God's creation." She had also had an art tutor who, as luck would have it, was a superb flower painter. He was George Cochran Lambdin (1830–1896), who specialized in the still-life depiction of roses and whose works are now housed in major US museum collections.

Mary also had relatives who wrote both fiction and journalism – a pastime regarded by her Quaker kin as being an appropriate outlet for a woman. As a writer, Mary directed her energies into travelogues and articles about alpine flora. In biographer Janice Sanford Beck's opinion, "Mary was particularly determined to convince other women that mountain adventures were not the male preserve she had once believed them to be."[7] And, as another sterling example of this inclination, there was her Philadelphian friend Mary Vaux Walcott, who, like Schäffer, roamed the backcountry of the Canadian Rockies annually and was a talented wildflower artist as well. (We will meet Vaux in the next chapter.)

Mary Schäffer records that drawing and then painting flowers to Charles's exacting standards was a lesson in itself, with many sketches ending up in the trash. By the time the couple were working together in such locales as Glacier (Rogers Pass), Field, Lake Louise and Banff, botanical illustration as an art genre had already reached, during the 18th and 19th centuries, what has been described as "the summit of perfection both artistically and technically."[8] Conceived, in the words of one scholar, as a "rigorously objective mirror of nature," in Mary's case this meant "that every petal, every stamen should be correct to the last [while sometimes] I was much more

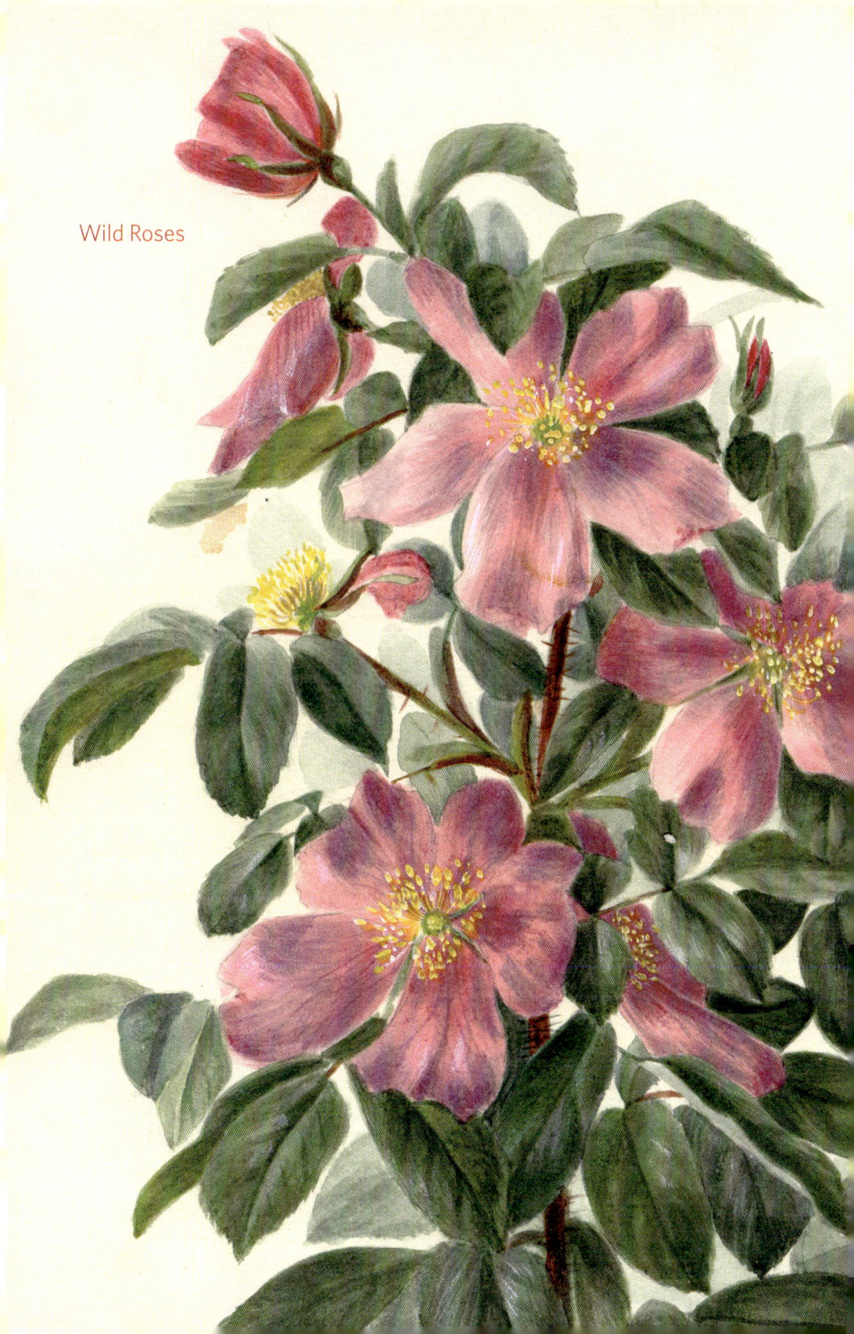
Wild Roses

interested in grouping…"[9] just as she had learned under Lambdin.

An example of a grouping is her *Prickly Rose*, depicted in enthusiastic bloom with its pinkish flowers and thick foliage. Sketched *in vivo*, the image implies a direct relationship with nature – an important feature of botanical art. Instead of being represented for symbolic purposes, as flowers had been for centuries in European art, or utilized as part of an aesthetically pleasing still-life for the Victorian parlour, *Prickly Rose* is treated as a botanical subject, despite its more casual, less detailed rendering.

Much more to Charles's liking, and closer to his idea of getting it "correct," is the crisper, more tightly controlled *Mountain Raspberry* (as identified in the bottom right-hand corner) or *Thimbleberry*, another member of the rose family. Here Schäffer is at her most detailed, displaying a remarkable sensitivity for the flower's varying shades and hues. The brownish rot on one leaf, for instance, is convincingly conveyed. In this watercolour, she also makes it perfectly understandable why *Rubus* (sp) *parviflorus*'s large, soft but sturdy, palmated leaves were used as liners for native baskets. The dainty white bloom, on the other hand, with its central core of yellow stamens, will, within a matter of a few days, be only a memory.

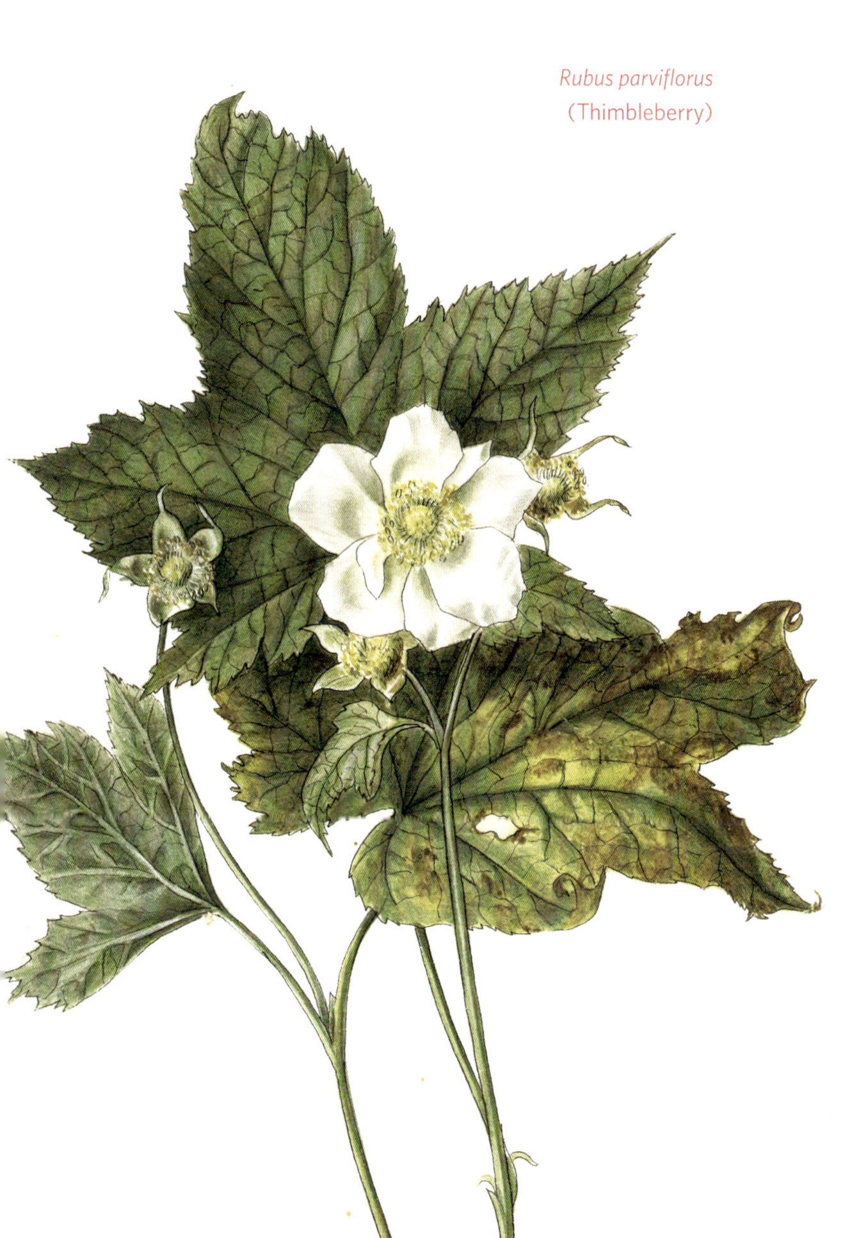

Rubus parviflorus
(Thimbleberry)

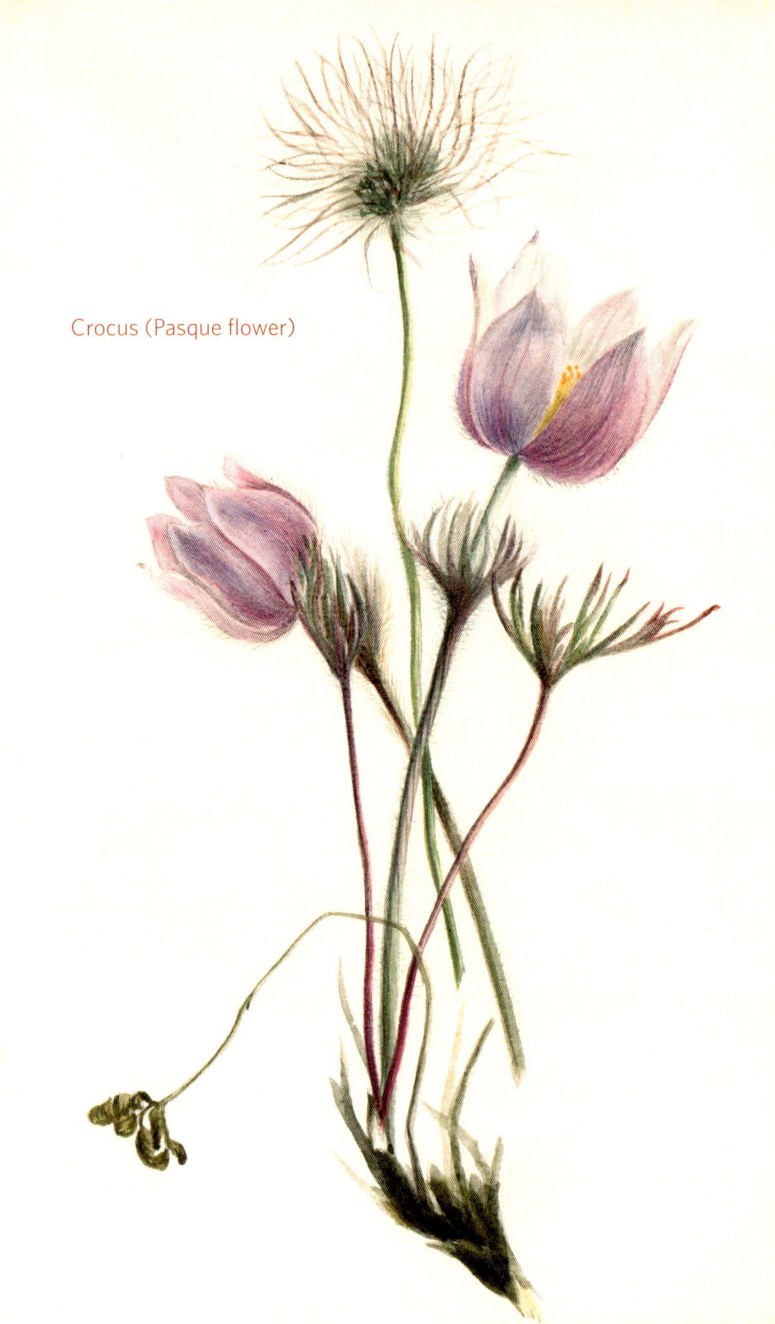

Crocus (Pasque flower)

The artistic approach Schäffer and her friend Mary Vaux Walcott adopted through their training, together with the expectations of botanists like Charles and the many examples of great botanical art from the past, is called *naturalism*. Based on the accurate description of people, places and things, naturalism as an approach did not imply merely passive reproduction of nature, nor was it simply a display of technical expertise. In the latter respect, neither of the two Marys' work could be called a remarkable example of "technique" when compared to painters such as France's Pierre-Joseph Redouté (1759–1840) or, much earlier, in Holland and far-off Suriname, Maria Sibylla Merian (1647–1717), but they did persevere with great focus and a willingness to work in tough outdoor conditions. Each work by each of the two Marys is unique and unrepeatable.

As seen in the soft pinks and mauves of the *Pasque Flower* – or, as it is more commonly known, the prairie crocus – Schäffer also excelled as a colourist. A welcome harbinger of spring ("pasque" being an old French word for Easter[10]), the season for this member of the buttercup family would be long gone by the time the artist recorded in her sketches the stronger reds of *Red Elderberry*, a type of honeysuckle whose berries are used for wine and jelly. Interestingly, as interpreted by the artist, these plants

Sambucus racemosa
(Red Elderberry)

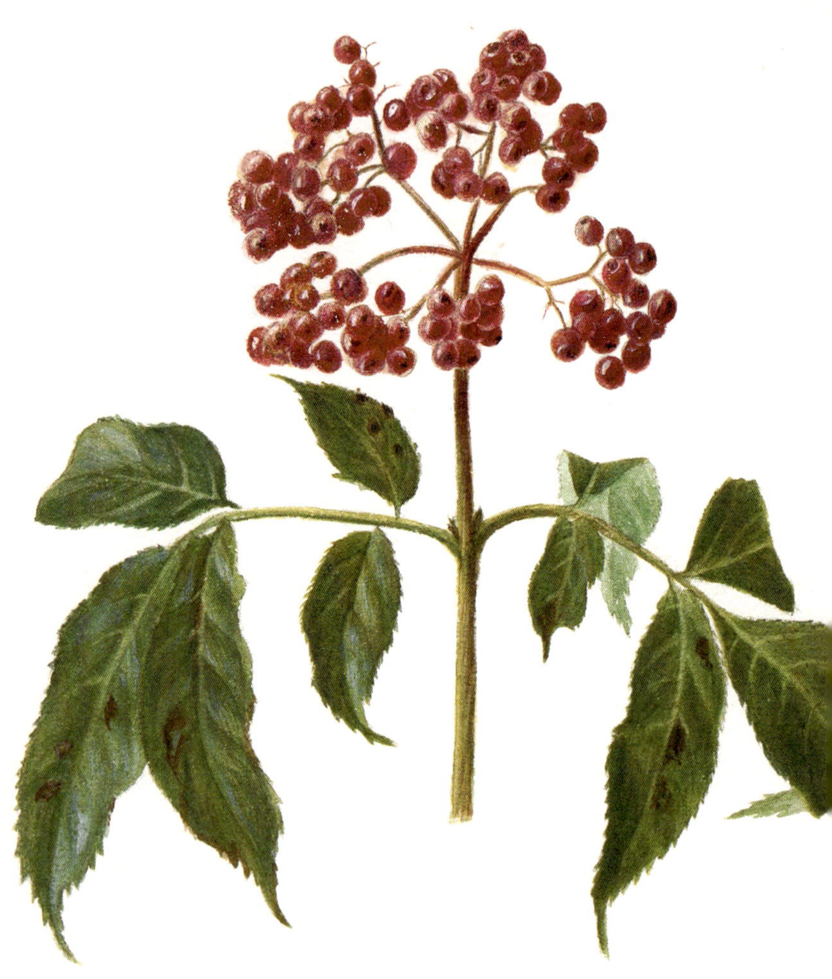

and many others by Schäffer appear totally detached from the demanding and sometimes hostile environment they inhabit. Instead, they seem to have come from another, more ethereal and delicate place.

Only three years set *Red Elderberry* (1903) apart from the rendering of *Pasque Flower* (1906), but between these two watercolours Schäffer's life had changed dramatically. In 1903 her beloved Charles had died of heart disease, followed quickly by the deaths of her mother and father. She was left not well off, but with the financial advice of Calgary lawyer and friend R.B. Bennett (later Prime Minister of Canada) and some nudging from Mary Vaux, Schäffer did go on to complete the illustrations for *Alpine Flora of the Canadian Rocky Mountains*.

Published in 1907 by G.P. Putnam's Sons and retailing for \$3 (the equivalent of about \$70 today),[11] the book was dedicated to Charles, with Stewardson Brown as the accredited author because Brown had finished the descriptions for his late friend. Significantly, it was in the process of finding and gathering even more new specimens for Brown that the annual "march of flowers" had taken Schäffer even farther into the wilderness. For her, in this second stage of working on the book, it meant getting used to riding a horse, camping in all kinds of weather and travelling in the company of men who were neither family nor spouse. One of the guides, a young Englishman named Billy Warren, would eventually become Mary's second husband and lifemate at "Tarry-a-while," a cottage-style home that still exists in Banff as an important heritage site.*

In all, a total of 163 plant species were identified and illustrated in *Alpine Flora of the Canadian Rocky Mountains*. But in a classic case of being beaten to the punch, this achievement was somewhat undermined, at least in Schäffer's mind, by the publication of another guidebook the year before, titled *Mountain Wildflowers of Canada*. The author was Julia Henshaw of Vancouver, who was not only a friend of Schäffer's but had also benefited from her colleague's wide knowledge of the subject. Still, where Henshaw was able to provide some very fine black and white photographs of various flora, Schäffer was also able to include her watercolours, showing, in effect, another side of her interpretative skills.

In 1911 Mary Schäffer returned to Maligne Lake to undertake, for the Canadian government, a more formal survey of this large, turquoise-coloured mountain gem. That same year, she also published an article in the journal of the Alpine Club of Canada, "Haunts of the Wild Flowers of the Canadian Rockies." Though much of her time was taken up by Maligne and her new book, *Old Indian Trails*

* Tarry-a-while is operated by the Whyte Museum of the Canadian Rockies.

of the Canadian Rockies, in the back of her mind the subject of wildflowers, so central to her deep connection to the alpine, was still a preoccupation. What she could not have predicted was how her own commitment to the uncovering of the rich flora of the Rockies would foreshadow the enthusiasms of so many others. As she noted in her journal article: "Few are those who climb throughout the Canadian mountains to whom the flowers of the region do not appeal. When twenty years ago there was one botanist searching hills and valleys, today there are fifty."[12] Of course, Mary Schäffer never considered herself a botanist, but "the garden" she so often spoke about, wrote about and illuminated in her art, made public in those early years a natural wonder that is still verdant and with us today.

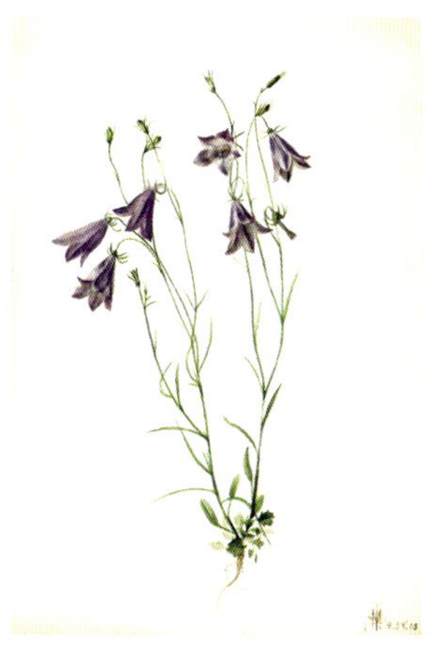

Campanula rotundifolia
(Harebell)

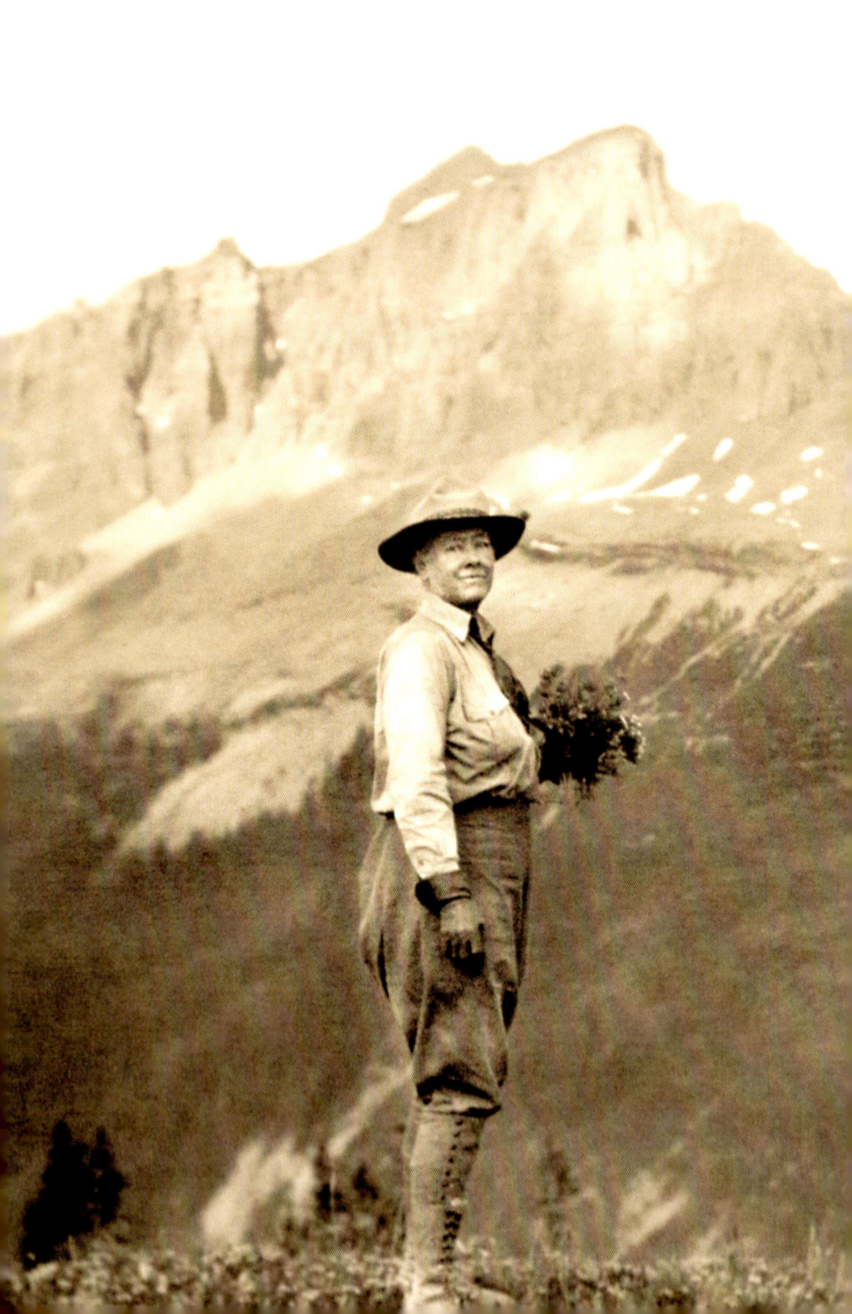

2

Mary Vaux Walcott
(1860–1940)

Mary Vaux Walcott and Mary Schäffer Warren had so much in common that it would have been amazing if their paths had never crossed. As it was, they knew each other from Philadelphia, a friendship based on an avid interest in the natural sciences, a love of art and photography and of course their Quaker heritage. A daughter of one of the oldest, wealthiest and most prominent Quaker families from "the city of brotherly love," Mary Morris Vaux (pronounced vox) was one year apart in birth – and, remarkably, one year apart in death – from Mary Schäffer. Of the two, Vaux was the first to set eyes on the Canadian Rockies, thanks to a trip on the country's new transcontinental rail line. Travelling in 1887* with her father,

* Schäffer would ride the Canadian Pacific westward two years later with her new husband, Charles Schäffer.

George, and brothers, George Jr. and William Jr., Mary had been impressed with the rugged, glaciated, alpine landscape of British Columbia and the western edge of the North-Western Territory (Alberta).

For the three siblings, the trip heralded the beginning of many summers spent in the western alpine, and for Mary in particular a lifelong commitment of over forty years to the area. To come were the pleasures of mountain rambling and backcountry camping in addition to the study of wildflowers and, on an entirely different scale, glaciers. As her grandnephew, Henry James Vaux, stressed to me, "Quakers didn't take vacations. You didn't do that. You were expected to be productive."[13] In the case of the youngest Vaux, William Jr., a trained engineer, this resulted quite naturally in the novel idea of investigating glaciers, especially the magnificent Great Glacier (Illecillewaet) in Rogers Pass, BC.

Located near the CPR hostelry called Glacier House, this icy, snow-packed behemoth was not difficult to reach, enabling the Vaux siblings to return each summer to measure and photograph the glacier's recession. The work was demanding, and Mary, who was technically trained,*

* William H. Rau, a professional photographer, had shown the family how to make fine platinum prints from the glass-plate negatives they brought back to Philadelphia.[14]

had the delicate job, in a tent, of developing negatives from the heavy, large-format cameras. The results were pioneering and even today, as a 2003 exhibition at Banff's Whyte Museum of the Canadian Rockies revealed, the crisp back and white photographs are still striking in their detail and information about climate change at the turn of the previous century.

As the exhibition's title – *Art Born of Science: The Vaux Family* – so evocatively expressed, there was more to these black and white platinum images so skilfully printed by Mary. In his book *Legacy in Ice: The Vaux Family and the Canadian Alps*, Edward Cavell takes note of the aesthetic handling of the hard-edged northern mountain light and the careful use of foreground to establish the subject. What's more, in some pictures there is a compositional flair for depicting the dramatic or the sublime, and in others a well-placed regard for the picturesque. Thus, looming next to where Mary Vaux stands is the impressive and towering toe of the colossal Illecillewaet Glacier.

In a more "anecdotal" moment but still surrounded by the primordial wilderness are long-skirted women sitting on the ground of a campsite – each with gloved hands holding a tea cup and saucer. Nothing out of place.

Like their friend Mary Schäffer, the Vauxes had a sense of the wilderness being a sacred place where, in the presence

Rocky Mountain Cassiope
(Western Mountain Heather)

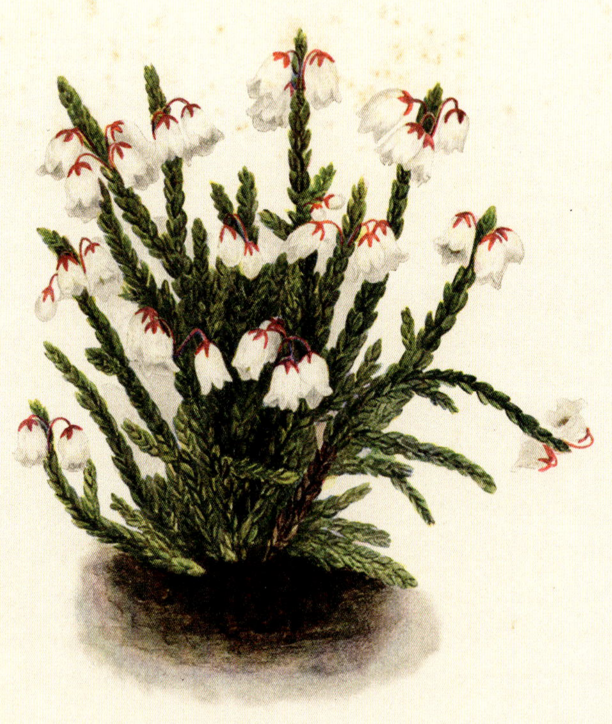

of "the Creator's handiwork," service in the name of science could be equated to the (Christian) "Almighty." And while Henry James Vaux, as a descendant, acknowledges the accomplishments of these early "amateur" glaciologists, he has always believed "they practised science basically as a guise to do their art. By doing that, they technically kept their [church] elders off their back."[15]

Documenting not only the glaciers in Rogers Pass but eventually those found in the Yoho, Lake Louise and Moraine Lake areas as well, the Vauxes explored the region with a curiosity and verve that had them scrambling to the tops of mountains, and in one case descending into the labyrinthine Nakimu Caves (Rogers Pass). The latter trip was notable for involving just the two Marys (Vaux and Schäffer), who, on their arduous trek to the caves, also found new native flower specimens.

In the same commercial spirit of providing free transportation to artists and photographers, Canadian Pacific gave the Vauxes free rail passes and guide service. In exchange, the family wrote and illustrated a publication about glaciers located along the CPR line. The 20-page pamphlet* was only one facet of how the Vauxes shared

* William and George Jr. are listed as the authors. Mary Vaux's contribution as the developer and printer of the pictures was usually signed with the family name only. The pamphlet was in circulation from 1900 to as late as 1922.

their keen enthusiasm for the West with their friends and colleagues.

In the winter months, their photographs were displayed for the clubs and societies in the East and lectures were illustrated with lantern slides – the PowerPoint of its day – prepared and painted by Mary Vaux. Philadelphia was a centre for science and culture in America, especially in the development of the photographic arts, and author Cyndi Smith suggests the family (Mary and George Jr.) were "forerunners in scenic photography, considering it a pleasing art form."[16] (Smith also thinks it's likely that Mary Schäffer learned her photographic skills from Mary Vaux.)

Nonetheless, such pursuits had to be tailored for their audience, because Quaker doctrine was not friendly to art as anything other than a means of illustration. Art as a creative outlet, as a form of personal expression, was frowned upon by Old Quakers as "vain and unnatural,"[17] according to Henry, who describes the Vaux family as being liberal. From a more contemporary perspective, Edward Cavell thinks the Vauxes' photographic achievement has as much to say about this day and age as it does about 19th-century enthusiasms for the natural world: "The era depicted is without today's feelings of environmental guilt. People were considered as an integral aspect of the wilderness, not interlopers."[18]

It seems that with every journey she made, Mary Vaux was pressing and painting wildflowers. It had been a subject dear to her heart even as a young girl, and in addition to watercolour it would later involve photography. Many years after Schäffer and Brown's 1907 reference book on alpine flora, Vaux published *North American Wild Flowers*, which, with 400 watercolours, covered the continent north of Mexico.* Published between 1925 and 1929, the five-volume work remains a stunning achievement, and not surprisingly Mary Vaux earned a reputation as the Audubon of the floral world. In her foreword, she tells the reader that in the "happy days of childhood," wild flowers were "a joy and an inspiration ... when I was taught to observe and sketch them under the direction of a skilled artist."[19]

* Vaux's illustrations of eastern and more southerly plants came from specimens given to her by others.

The name of that artist is not known, but in the collection of the Smithsonian American Art Museum the earliest work by Vaux is a watercolour of two pink pansy-like flowers titled simply *My First Painting*. The date of the work is 1868, making the artist eight years old. By her late teens, Vaux was making watercolours that look very accomplished. Most of the works are untitled but all appear to be native flowers. Poignantly, the last work in the collection

Lake Louise Arnica

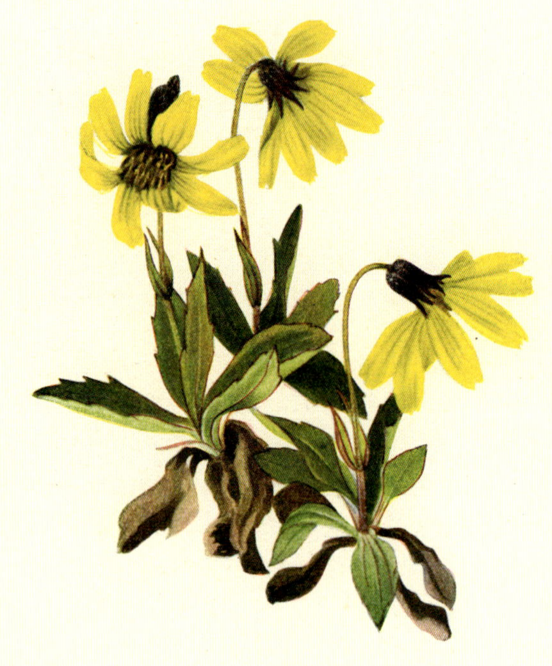

is also an untitled flower study, completed in 1940, the year she died. Apparently, Mary Vaux painted thousands of watercolours and had the ability to paint directly from the subject, without a pencil sketch.

In her groundbreaking book *Off the Beaten Track: Women Adventurers and Mountaineers in Western Canada*, Cyndi Smith provides a vivid description of how in hobnail boots and knickerbockers, or plus-fours (Mary's preference), this "lady" pursued her craft:

> When traveling by horseback Mary carried her paint box and pads on the back of her saddle, and her camera boxes over the pommel. Sometimes she would paint by a fire to keep her stiffened fingers warm. At other times she would bring the flowers back to camp, where she would re-arrange them in water and paint them in better light.[20]

Despite the rigours of working outdoors and living in camp for weeks at a time, it may seem like Mary Vaux had somewhat of a carefree life. But, as a descendant of Mary's brother George, a lawyer, Henry James Vaux thinks it was actually difficult for her to pursue her interests.[21] With the death of her mother, Sarah, "Miss Mary Vaux," at age twenty the eldest child and only daughter, was obliged to take care of the family farm, the household

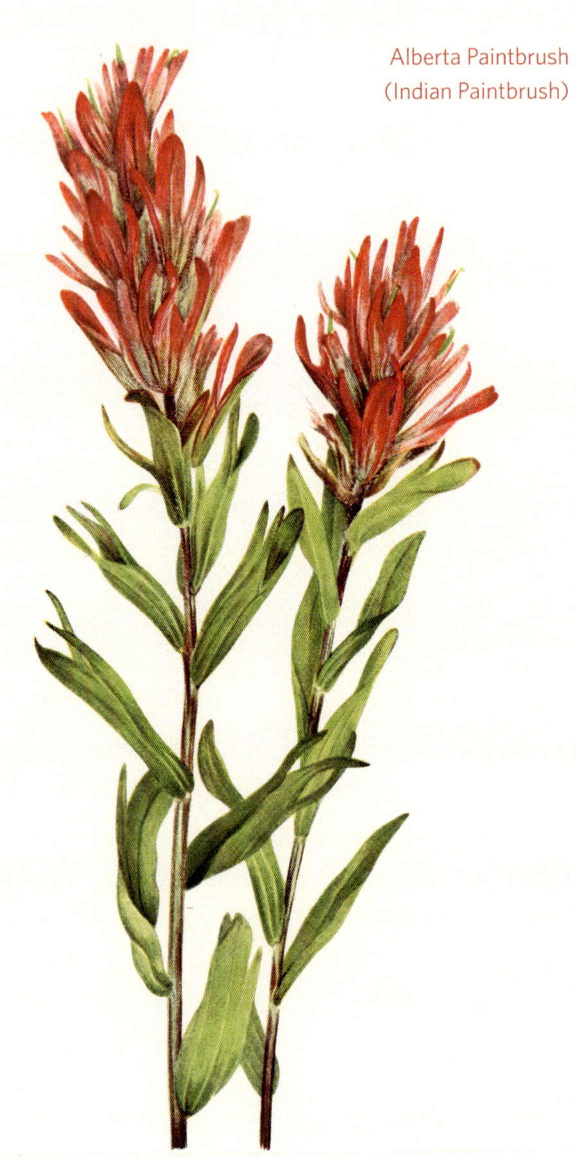

Alberta Paintbrush
(Indian Paintbrush)

in Philadelphia and her father, who stopped talking to her thirty-four years later when she changed her surname and moved to Washington, DC, in 1914. There, at age 54, she joined Dr. Charles Doolittle Walcott (1850–1927), who was then the head of the Smithsonian Institution. By all reports, it couldn't have been a more congenial match, with marriage representing a kind of liberation for Vaux. Once married, the compulsion for painting and photographing native plants transformed itself into a study worthy of a professional's respect.

Significantly, Walcott himself also had strong connections to the Rockies and especially its Cambrian geology and fossils. He is credited with discovering the Burgess Shale, on Mount Wapta in Yoho National Park, one of the most important fossil fields of early animal life and now a UNESCO World Heritage Site. Beginning in 1915 the couple established a summertime routine, spending three to four months in the West, Charles preoccupied with geology and fossils and Mary intent on gathering the best floral specimens possible, representing, as she wrote for her magisterial book, "the natural grace and beauty of the plant without conventional design."

In her case this meant a boldly stated style of depiction, very unlike the delicacy of a Mary Schäffer wildflower. For Mary Vaux, native plants appear as hardy, living

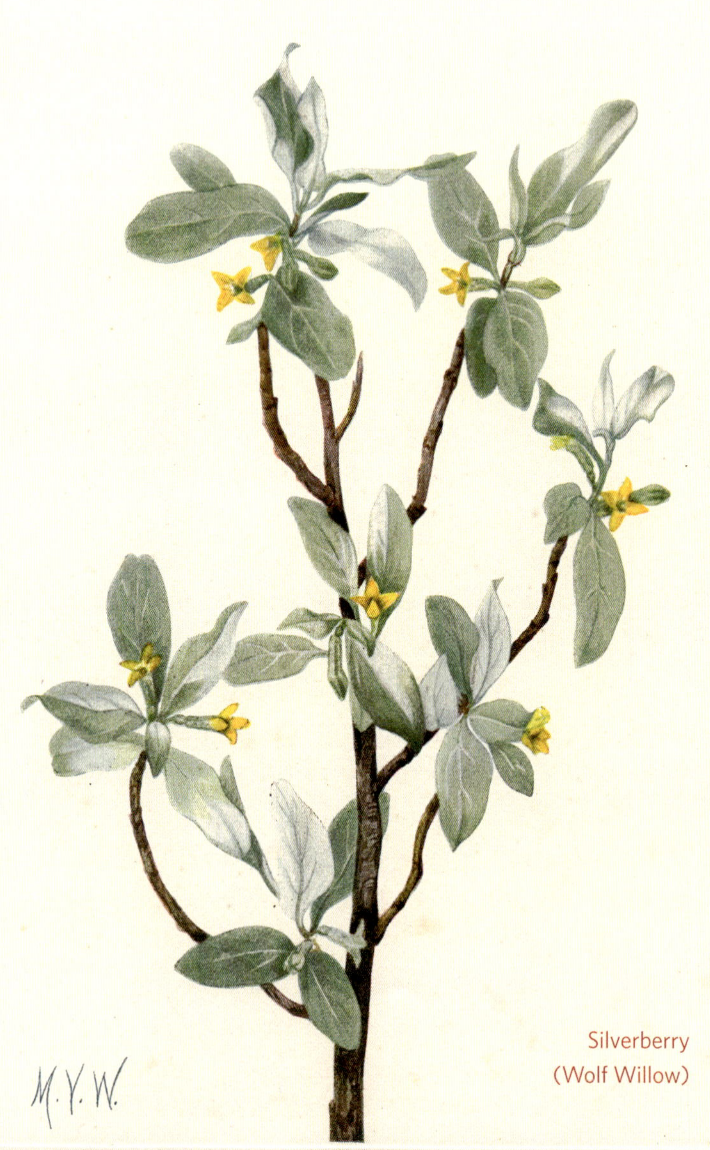

Silverberry
(Wolf Willow)

things, no matter how tiny the bloom or slender the stalk. The upright, sun-seeking *Alberta Paintbrush** and the much rarer and smaller *Lake Louise Arnica* are examples of this approach. Constrained as they are to the shortest growing season possible, the existence of such flora is all the more amazing. They are, as Mary Vaux interprets them, survivors perfected by adversity.

The artist herself wrote the short descriptions for each plant, including where the particular specimen was obtained. For the gorgeous but parasitic** *Alberta Paintbrush*, she writes that it was collected at "an altitude of 6,500 feet," "near our camp on the headwaters of the Clearwater River, forty-five miles by trail north of Lake Louise." In all, with Walcott and the guides, Mary covered more than five thousand miles of terrain before the completion of *North American Wild Flowers*. Strikingly, a few trees and shrubs were also included in the five-volume work, "with the hope that these exquisite forms may be more observed and appreciated by nature lovers." It was a wise decision, and two favourites of mine are included here, the watercolours *Silverberry* and *Western Larch*.

* Popularly known as Indian paintbrush or common red paintbrush.

** Parasitic because the flowers attach to other plants, making this species nearly impossible to transplant to the garden.

The silverberry, better known where I live as wolf willow, is a tall shrub and a member of the oleaster family rather than the willow family. They're hard to miss as you're walking along on an open trail in the early summer. There is its distinctive greenish-grey leaf covered in minuscule silvery scales and tiny yellow flowers smelling all cloying and sweet. In the fall, the natives would gather the berry-like seeds for necklaces and decoration on clothes.

Alberta's Bow Valley, home to Lake Louise, Banff and Canmore, is also home to what amounts to an annual autumn hiking ritual that is inextricably bound up with genus *Larix*, the larch. For first-time visitors and friends, it's the most unusual tree they will see, a conifer that actually drops its old needles in the fall and grows new ones in the spring. Both events are accompanied by the most heavenly colour: a vivid shade of pale green at the start of a new growing season and an equally rich gold at the end. Better yet, the needles are soft to the touch, and as the tree ages, its bark becomes deeply furrowed and dark in colour. Even a single tree contains the most stunning contrasts. Put a whole bunch of them together in a stand and you have an annual fall pilgrimage of larch lovers marching to the higher terrain.

Three species of *Larix* exist in North America. The western larch, represented by Vaux, is a more symmetrical

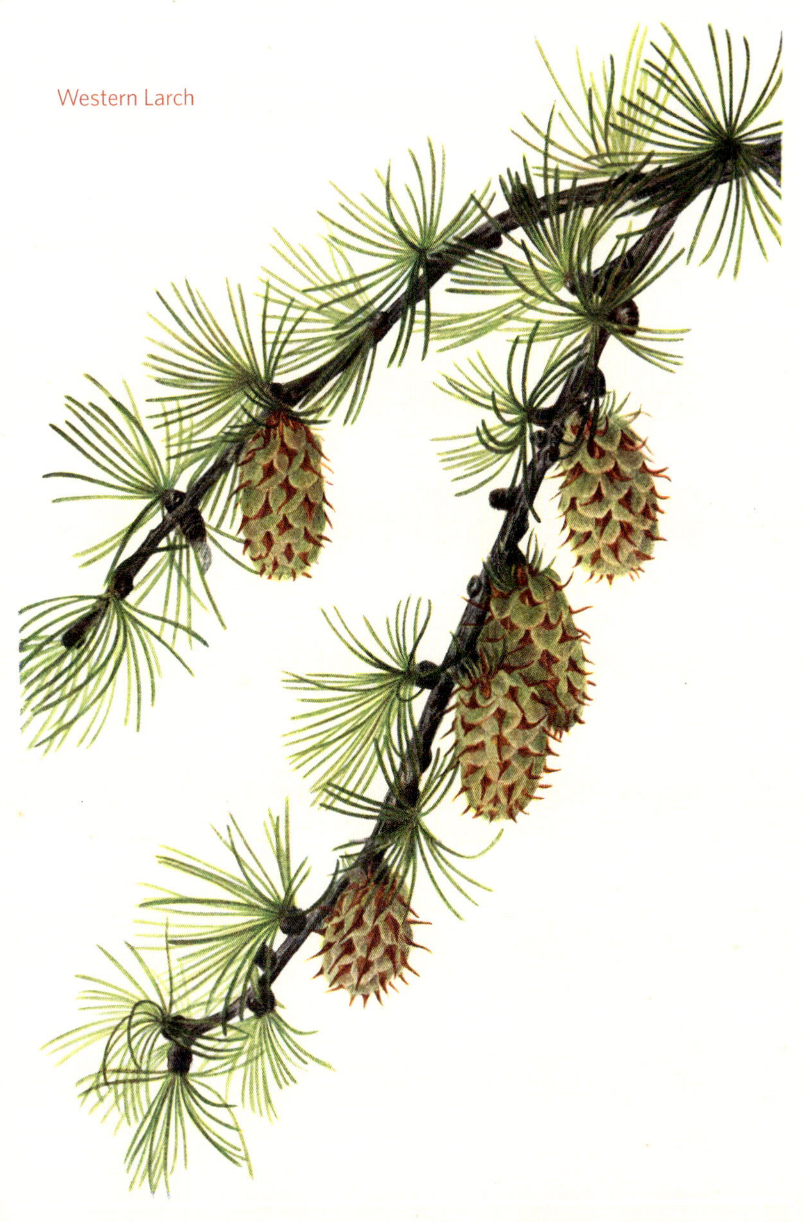
Western Larch

species that grows at a lower elevation than the subalpine larch of the Bow Valley. Found by the artist alongside a tributary of the Columbia River in BC, its cones – in contrast to the clusters of light, feathery needles – are spiny-looking creatures, their woody scales protected by pointy red bracts. The artist describes the larger western larch as a stately tree and expresses concern for the large numbers that are cut every year for railway ties.

Though *North American Wild Flowers* was published by the Smithsonian, Vaux actually spent several years selling subscriptions and raising money to cover the costs of printing in colour. A colour publication may seem commonplace today but in the 1920s the expense and labour required for such an undertaking "pushed the printing industry to such heights that for years the methods used were known as the Smithsonian process."[22] By the time volume five appeared in 1929, an amazing $750,000 had gone into the effort, the equivalent of about US$9.9-million today.[23]

The work received rave reviews, not only for its colour reproductions but also for its botanically accurate and artistically engaging treatment of flowering and non-flowering plants. There was, as well, the interesting matter of the lists found at the front of each volume. An index of flowers introduced the reader to a subject where common names are sometimes the most memorable thing about the plant, while a patron's list illuminated Mary Vaux Walcott's own social status, married as she was to one of the most important scientific names in America of the time. Recognizable even today were names such as DuPont, Carnegie, Rockefeller – all patrons with ties to industrial wealth. Other donors were the National Geographic Society and the Library of Congress as well as commercial giants such as Eli Lilly & Co. and the Canadian Pacific Railway. Girl Scouts Incorporated was also part of the roll call of 174 patrons.

More likely to provoke a smile, though, was each volume's index of flowers. With common names such as spotted beebalm, johnny jump-up, tar-flower, lambkill, buff pussytoes and beautyberry, each one contains a nugget of whimsy and social history. Not seen in the West but actually collected as a specimen near Mary Vaux's winter home in Washington, DC, were the sweet blue Quaker ladies, from the provocatively named madder family (*Rubiaceae*).

In every sense, Mary Vaux's contribution to recording and conveying the wonder of this fascinating subject was larger in scale, in number and ultimately in impact than that of her lifelong friend Mary Schäffer. In 1936, four years before her death, the veteran adventurer had no problem attracting 2,000 people in Toronto to hear

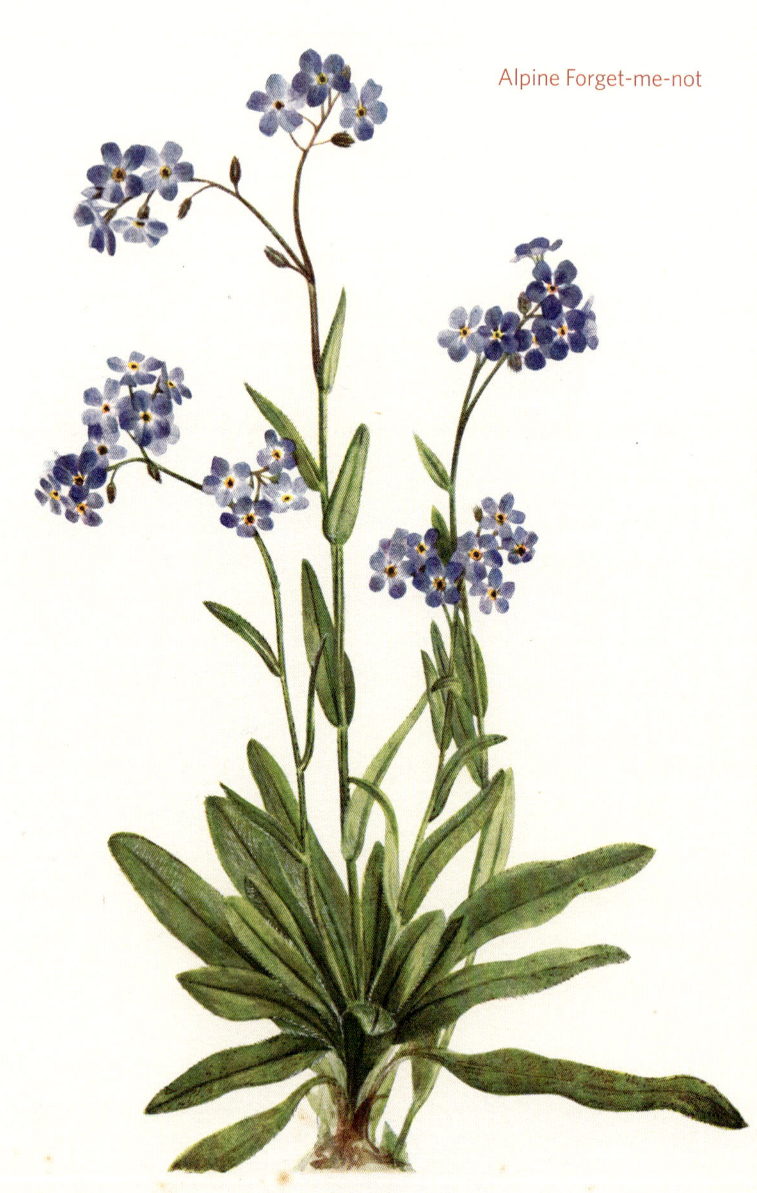

Alpine Forget-me-not

her speak about wildflowers. As an encyclopedic work, *North American Wild Flowers* has also resurfaced twice in the last century, its most recent incarnation as a miniature book – this in contrast to Mary Schäffer's much earlier achievement, *Alpine Flora of the Canadian Rocky Mountains*, which has never been reprinted.

Nonetheless, both women can stand shoulder to shoulder, because as Cyndi Smith notes, "Even though the mountains were only a few days' train journey away from major Canadian cities, Canadians were not the ones who flocked to them to explore and climb – rather, Europeans and Americans were the takers."[24] By the time Schäffer and Vaux appeared on the scene, western Canada was a place of settlement and colonization, and probably for many eastern Canadians a place of uncomfortable extremes and contrasts. A hinterland.

More broadly, the urge to "go look at the mountains," as historian Terry Abraham puts it,[25] was barely a popular idea anywhere in the world before the 1800s, and as circumstances would have it, along with a pertinent amount of Victorian and Quaker-bred curiosity, both women rode the crest of a new sensibility and wonder about the higher reaches of the planet. Luckily for us, they, as artists, chose to look downward at the nature around their feet.

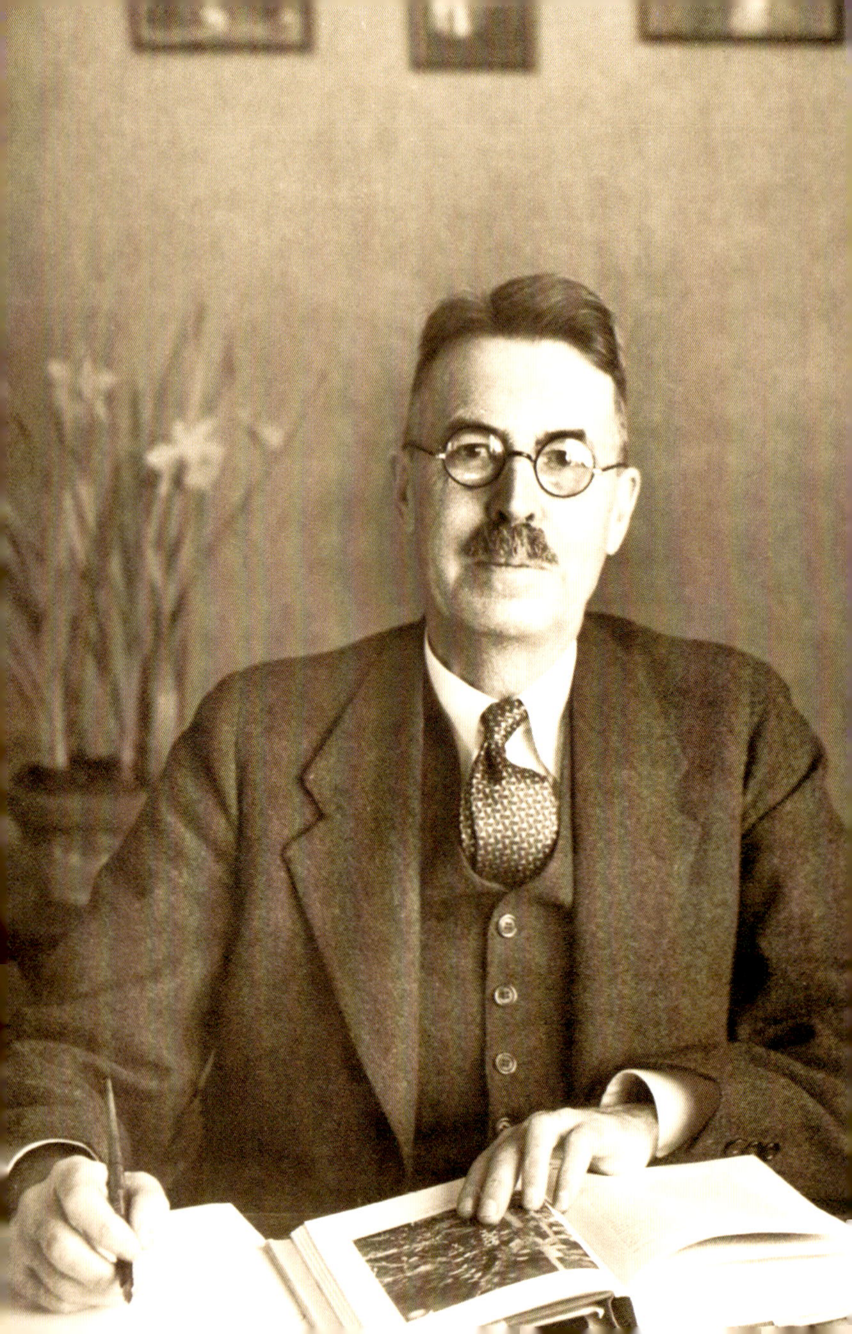

3

William Copeland McCalla
(1872–1962)

William (Will) Copeland McCalla is the most atypical of the six artists represented here. In his ninety years, chances are that this farmer, educator, naturalist and author never considered his photographs as art. This despite being exasperated by the oft-made comment "My, you must have a good camera!"[26] To which the answer would be, Yes, he did: a Zeiss with an *f*3.5 lens and double extension bellows designed to produce close up photos of the smallest of plants. But even with such professional equipment for its time, how to account for the remarkable results: native flora made all the more vivid, luminous and memorable because of how they were arranged, photographed and then presented to his audience in the form of hand-coloured lantern slides projected on a wall or screen.

It's only with the passage of time that this bespectacled

Canadian of Scottish descent looks all the more like an artist with one foot planted firmly in the world of botany and the other in that more nebulous area where a finely tuned aesthetic sensibility makes for an engaging piece of art no matter what the picture's scientific value may be. A pioneer in the discovery and recording of wild plants of the prairie provinces, William Copeland McCalla did for the prairies what Mary Schäffer Warren and Mary Vaux Walcott did for the mountains. This included a huge body of photographic works and a book, *Wild Flowers of Western Canada*[27] – the first of its kind for the prairie region. There are no watercolours included in this legacy – only hundreds of enlarged photographs of native plants, of which over 1,400 were donated years ago to the National Museum of Natural Sciences (Canadian Museum of Nature) in Ottawa. An extensive collection of hand-painted lantern slides now resides in the Provincial Archives of Alberta in Edmonton, and it is from this latter collection that the McCalla images in this book are reproduced.

Like the older Mary Schäffer and Mary Vaux, McCalla, as an easterner, also had the urge to "go look at the mountains," something he first achieved in 1899 when he travelled to Banff from his home in Ontario. Like many others before him with a bent for painting or photographing this special place, his transportation cost was covered by Canadian Pacific in exchange for photographs. According to the family history,[28] McCalla camped for two months and brought back botanical specimens then new to science. Three of these – a willow, a *draba* (a type of flowering grass) and a dainty primrose – were named after him. By happy coincidence, Mary Schäffer too was aware of this dainty springtime denizen commonly known as bird's-eye primrose and at some point made a lovely lantern slide of it titled *Primula McCallian*.*

It's tantalizing to imagine the ramblings of these three dedicated hunters of flora – McCalla, Schäffer and Vaux – taking place in the same summer. At the time, Vaux was still in the routine of studying glaciers with her two brothers, painting wildflowers and climbing mountains, while Schäffer was working diligently with her husband, Charles, at collecting and photographing botanical specimens. Did their paths cross with this younger man's? Did these two mountain mistresses share with him information about where the best alpine meadows could be found or which scree slopes of the higher terrain had the most varied dwarf-size perennials? No one seems to know.

* Several decades later, this flower was identified as being the same as a species first documented in Quebec as *Primula mistassinaca*. Nonetheless, the title of the Schäffer work bears the McCalla name.

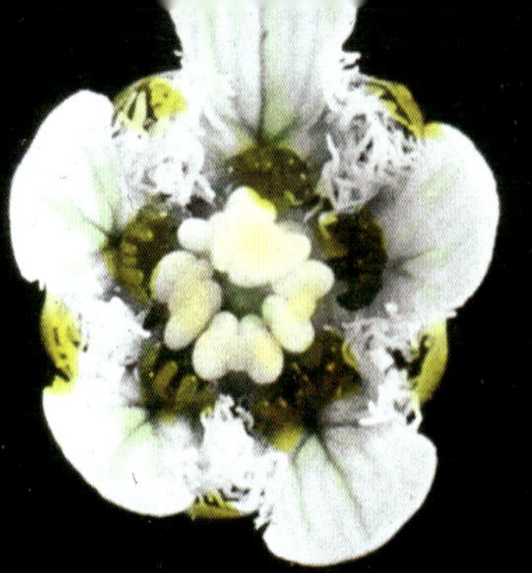

Movements of Floral Parts: *Parnassia fimbriata*: Showing how stamens expand one by one

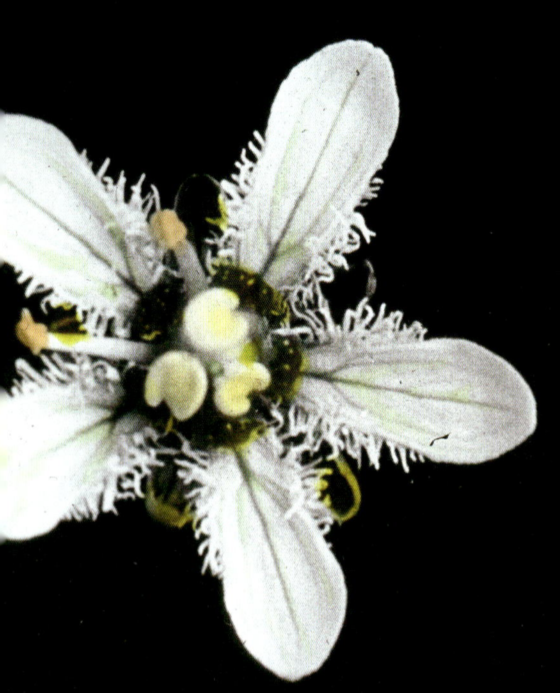

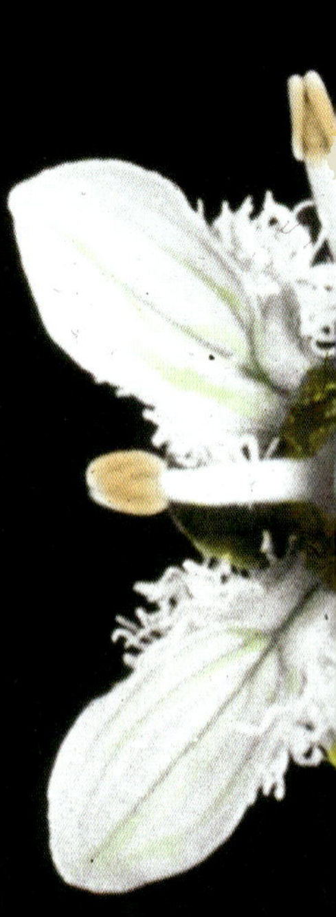

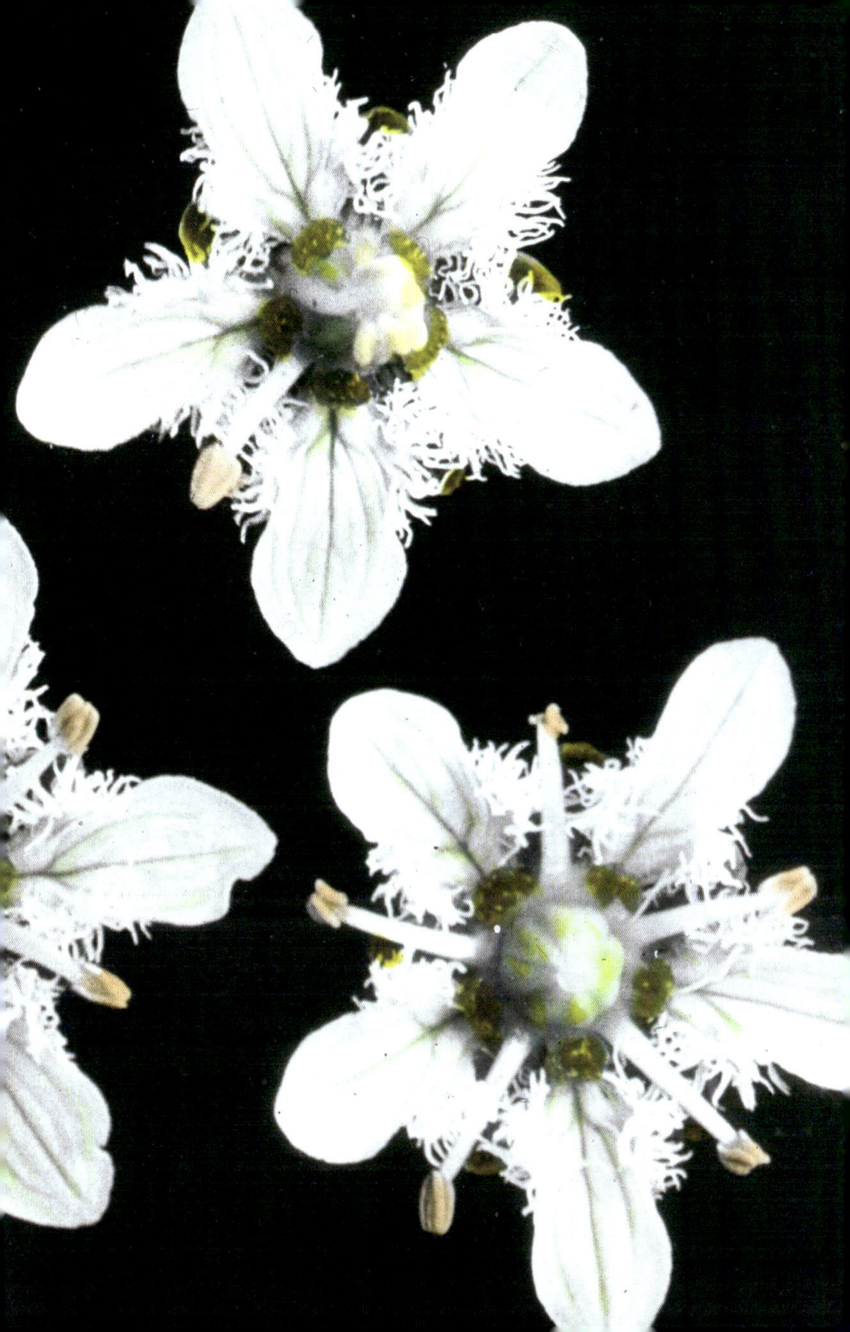

Born in St. Catharines, Ontario, to a prominent family, McCalla had a green thumb from an early age. The family business was groceries and hardware, but more attractive to the teenage boy was his father's conservatory, where there were plants to be cared for. McCalla was meticulous by nature and well suited to any task involving the details of note-taking and record-keeping. What he was not endowed with was good health. He suffered from eye trouble and, worse for any plant lover, asthma. He enjoyed photography, too, and saddled as he was with bad eyes and a compromised respiratory system, it would have required extra persistence to pursue either avocation well. In the early 1890s he tried to study botany at Cornell University but lasted only one term because of health problems. Alas, as part of McCalla's life narrative, the issue of asthma was always somewhere in the background, including being the impetus for his eventual decision to move west for a drier and hopefully healthier climate.

By then it was early 1913, which meant not only moving his wife, Margaret Ratcliffe, and their seven children, ages ten to two, but also selling his beloved "Sunny Acres," a fine fruit and vegetable farm just outside St. Catharines. McCalla had had great success as a grower and is described in the family history as a "scientific

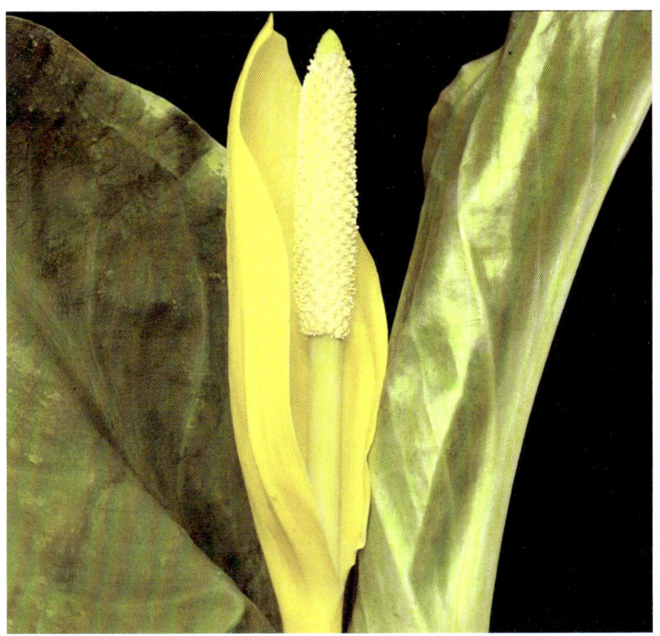

Lysichiton camtschatcense – Western Skunk Cabbage

farmer, well ahead of his time."[29] He had also taken to photographing the bounty of Sunny Acres and had a flair for creating displays of the farm's produce. In one 1909 picture, at least six varieties of squash are arranged in a standing pyramid form. It is a delightful arrangement and suggests McCalla knew intuitively how to create an appealing composition. Not surprisingly the squash display won first prize at a local horticultural fair. McCalla was also not adverse to taking short courses on botany and giving talks to farmers about soil fertility, fruit growing and pruning, as well as producing for fruit and tomato processors in southwestern Ontario. In addition, though McCalla's time at Cornell may have been short-lived, Roger Vick of Edmonton's Devonian Botanic Garden notes the influence of the renowned American botanist and taxonomist Dr. Liberty Hyde Bailey,[30] a leader in the progressive Country Life Movement.

Spurred by the promise of an improved, more wholesome life in the newly settled areas of the American and Canadian West, from all appearances Will and Margaret McCalla couldn't have been more in sync with the spirit of the Country Life Movement. Educated, resourceful, fully engaged with family and rural life – able to "stand on their own two feet," as the saying goes – they had already proven themselves in the fertile countryside of central Canada, and thus they brought with them all the attributes and energies needed for a less developed region like western Canada. For a short while, their new home was Edmonton, where McCalla and a partner went into the business of building houses. It was during Alberta's first construction boom, and as so many would discover, any hopes of doing well in real estate can disappear as quickly as any rainbow. By the time the guns began firing in Europe, in August 1914, the

McCalla family, after a false start in Edmonton, were back to farming – this time on an unfinished homestead called Glenbrook Farm.

Despite the farm's pastoral name, Will and Margaret were now really pioneers on the frontier. They located only 14 miles east of Edmonton, in the Bremner district, but settled during a period when the climate seemed to be more inclement than normal. Their plans of running a vegetable market garden with some additional fields of wheat were undermined from year one. As always, McCalla was attentive to keeping a log, and his notes from this period can be a depressing read. If it wasn't a late, killing frost wiping out the green beans on July 3, it was cutworms killing off, in just 36 hours, 240 of 325 cabbages planted. And then, in 1915, there was the great potato crop badly infected with scab. Throw into that mix the mercurial appearances of the chinook, even this far north, with its strange powers to change the temperature from a bitter –43°C to a slushy +7°C in a single day, and the pioneer lament about toil and tribulation seems far too real in the McCalla case.

Glenbrook Farm remained in the McCalla family until 1966, with Fred, the oldest son, taking over the operation as it shifted to raising livestock and grain. After a six-year absence, Will's asthma returned in 1918, and from there it was only a matter of time before he began to seek not just other employment but a whole new calling. In 1926, after finding temporary work as a librarian at the Edmonton Normal School, McCalla, Margaret and the younger children moved to Calgary, where Will took up a position teaching natural history, again at the Normal School. At last the avocations of botany and photography became part of McCalla's paid occupation as this committed individual undertook to train hundreds of student teachers in what Euripides – a philosopher he admired and quoted – called "the secrets of the earth."

To that job McCalla would bring a substantial collection of carefully pressed plants in herbarium sheets, black and white photographs, and the already published *Wild Flowers of Western Canada*. Featuring sixty pictures, most likely developed at Glenbrook, where a dugout cellar served as one of McCalla's darkrooms, the reference book was a remarkable achievement. Intended for the general public, the work is not about "pretty" flowers to pick, but about those that are common to the landscape, with additional descriptions of the environments that sustain them. Writing, for instance, about the Western woodland, McCalla commented about how its shady environs have "a tranquilizing and restorative effect upon the mind."[31] He noticed, as well, that woodland flora are "smoother and broader of leaf, more delicately coloured and generally more graceful than their kinsmen of the plains."[32]

McCalla takes a holistic look at his subject, reminding his readers, in another case, that although the western wood lily "may be seen in great bunches packed into vases, cans or pails"[33] in rural homes and schools, they "should be the heritage of mankind for all time, but the choicest are in danger of disappearing in a single generation." A copy of the 1920 book was provided free of charge to every school in Alberta* and much to my surprise, ninety years later, I obtained a copy of *Wild Flowers of Western Canada* from the regional library system where I live. The book's spine was a little worse for wear, but I can imagine it residing at one time in the local school library, serving as one of the few books of its time that was about this place, western Canada.

Photographically, some of the black and white images bring to mind the art of Berlin photographer Karl Blossfeldt (1865–1932), who was renowned for his close-up photographs of plants. McCalla's subjects too are sharply focused and carefully arranged against a dark screen, and he is clearly inspired by the way plants grow and the shapes and forms they take. While his groupings

* Roger Vick has proposed the Alberta Department of Education was most likely involved with the book's publication.

of plants may not be as sculptural in form or aesthetically fine-tuned as those of the turn-of-the-century German, there is no doubt about their singularity and presence as a force of nature. They stand tall and are revealed in all their odd but purposeful variety and sometimes strange detail. McCalla continued his botany/photography expeditions later in life, and grandson Dennis McCalla recalls family memories of children "being commandeered to help, often by holding screens or reflectors to direct more light on the subject."[34] "Mosquitoes often proved a torment," Dennis writes, suggesting first-hand experience.

In addition to taking hundreds of student teachers on field trips, from 1926 to 1938 when he retired, McCalla made nearly a thousand lantern slides, not just of flora but of animal and insect life and the varied environments of the prairie landscape. They are astonishing for their colour, luminous light and composition. Photographed against a black velvet background, the distinctive shapes of the robust and messy vegetal world are revealed in all their startling and elegant forms.

With his *Dandelion Heads in Fruit, Open and Closed*, even a ubiquitously ho-hum plant is taken to another level of reality, depicted as much for its formal beauty as for its familiar, everyday form. I couldn't help but think of the later floral studies of the acclaimed American photographer

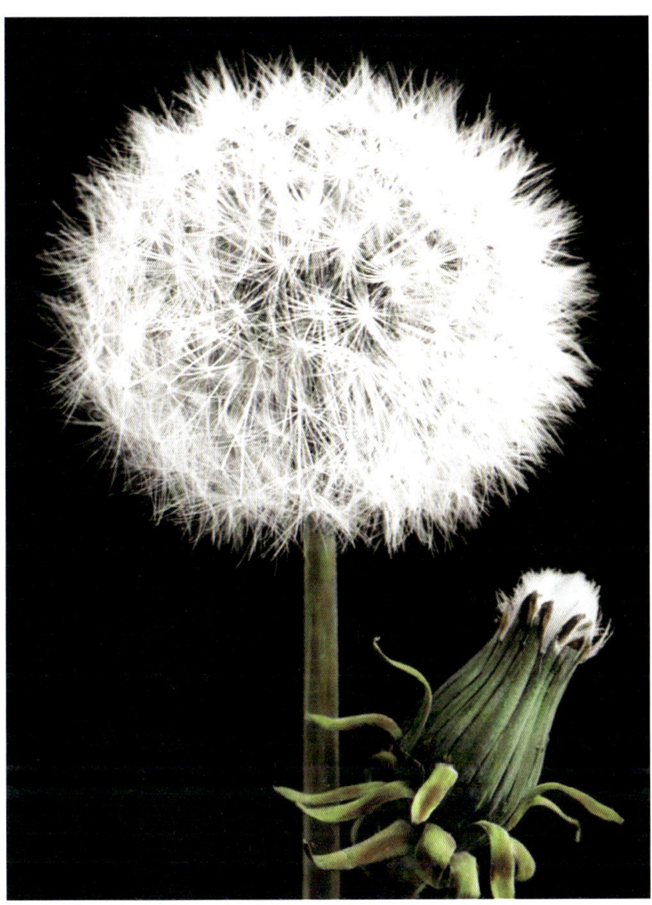

Dandelion heads in fruit, open and closed

Robert Mapplethorpe (1946–1989). Likewise revealed in all its particularity and rareness is the fringed pinesap, in

McCalla's slide *Indian Pipe.* Possibly photographed in the shaded, moist poplar woods of the Cypress Hills, this demure-looking, difficult to find, flowering perennial lives without chlorophyll, feeding on decaying organic matter. Lucidly evoked by McCalla in its rich and textured humus surroundings, there is little wonder that another common name for this solitary plant is ghost flower.

Monotropa hypopitys – Many Flowered Indian Pipe

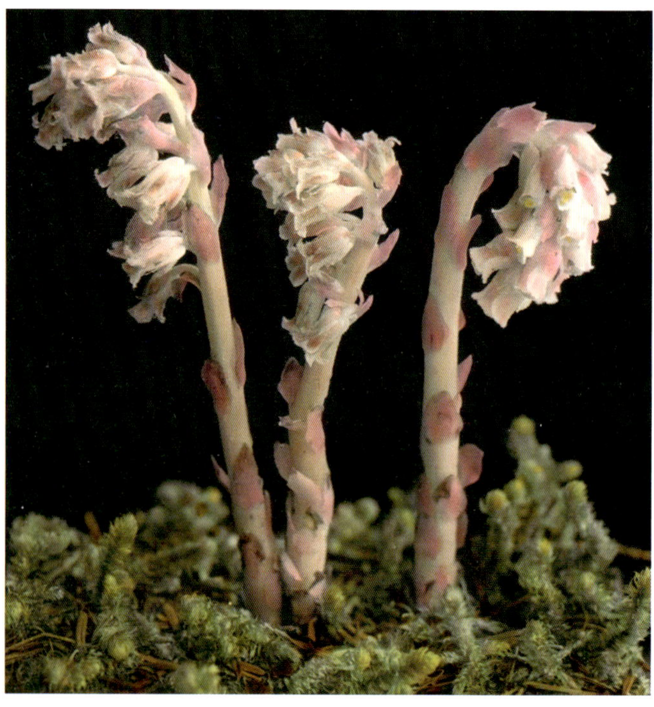

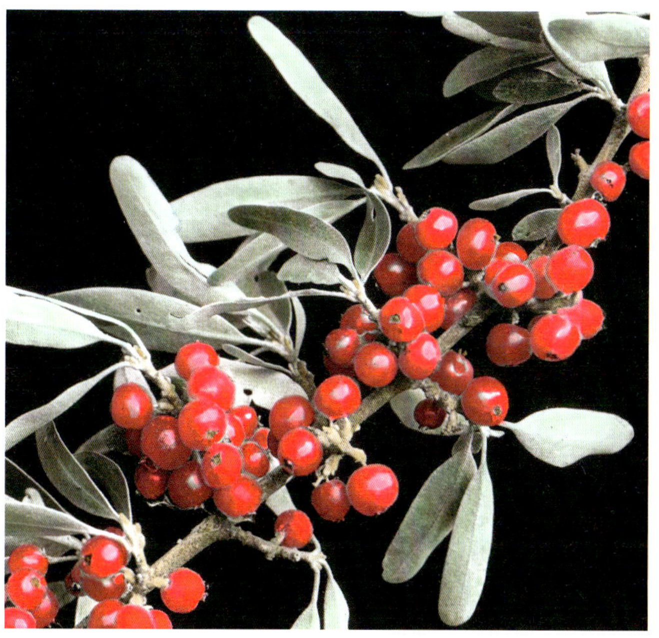

Shepherdia argentea – Buffalo Berry

If the double extension bellows attached to the camera enabled the photographer to capture his subjects' form and textures at a larger scale, only his eye and a meticulous sense of colour were responsible for their chromatic intensity. The sumptuous red of *Buffalo Berry* is a marvel when one considers that this image began as a black and white photo on sheet film which was then printed on a 3¼″ × 4″ glass plate to be coloured and tinted by brush. For *Indian Pipe* as well, McCalla used a good-size magnifying glass and a Kodak product called Velox Transparent Watercolour Stamps, along with an elaborate colour chart.[35]

The buffaloberry is a shrub of medium height, sometimes called shepherdia in the area where I live, and it is easy to understand why bears are attracted to the fruit of this abundant plant. The berries practically advertise themselves, clustered as they are like petite grapes on a vine. Photographed at an angle, everything about this image seems in place. Given its clarity and colour purity, this picture is as fresh as yesterday. In contrast is the lantern slide McCalla made of a tall, outstanding plant found in the Rockies south of Crowsnest Pass and used extensively by aboriginal peoples. Titled *Bear Grass (Glacier Park)*, the image shows a big patch of this lily plant in bloom and has

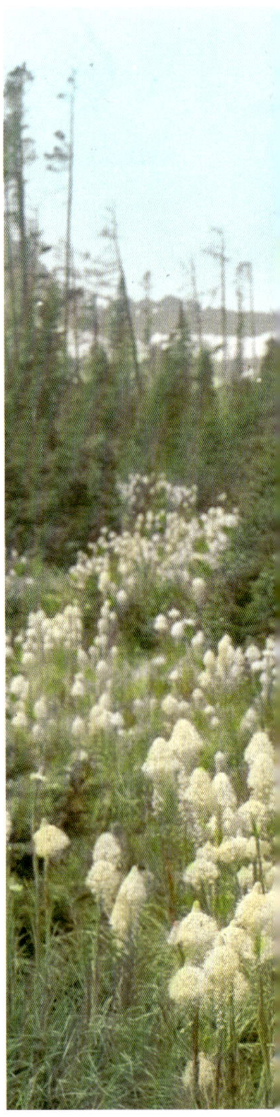

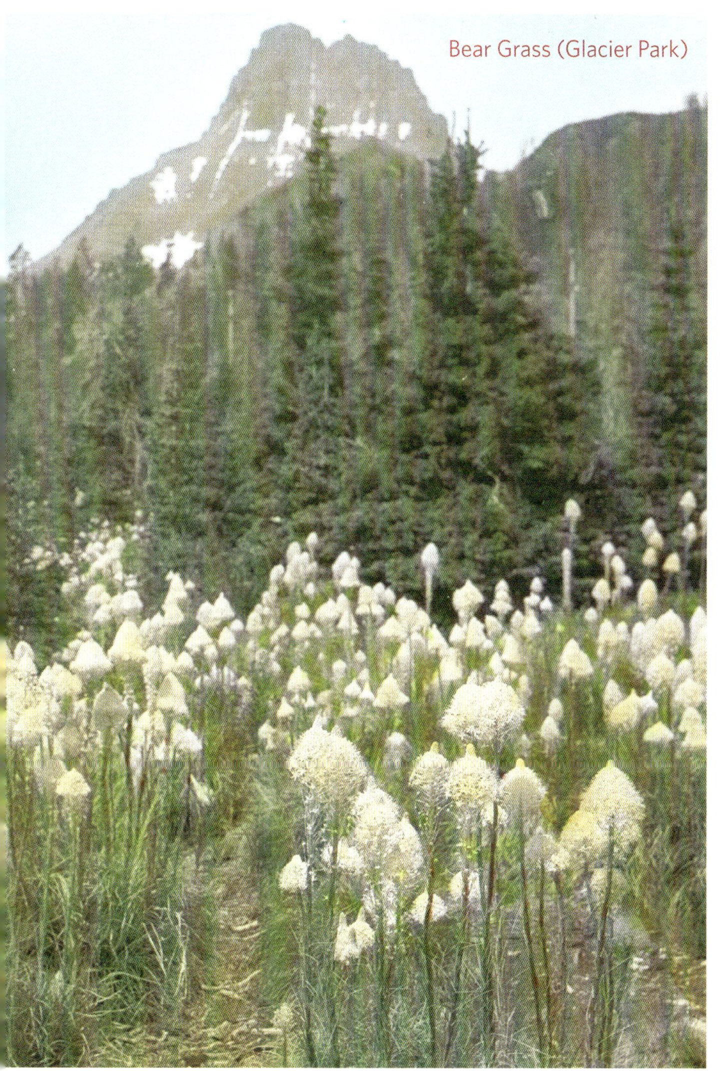
Bear Grass (Glacier Park)

the bygone appearance of the hand-coloured postcards people now collect.

Following his retirement, William Copeland McCalla devoted more of his time to his botanical studies. (How could he not!) He became a respected authority on the flora of western Canada and in 1956 received an honorary degree from the University of Alberta. The subject he had wanted to study 50 years earlier at Cornell had, over time, found its own way into his life and, quite naturally, that of Margaret, who assisted him in the work. Dennis remembers how, at family get-togethers, a "humongous projector" would illuminate the lantern slides in a darkened room. Such shows, whether seen by family, students or the public, would usually begin with a slide of the Canadian flag followed by a beautifully handwritten quote from Euripides. Projected on the wall or screen, the quote read:

> Happy the man whose lot it is to know
> The secrets of the earth. He hastens not
> To work his fellow's hurt by unjust deeds,
> But with rapt admiration contemplates
> Immortal nature's ageless harmony,
> And how and when her order came to be.

McCalla was one such man, expressing his "rapt admiration" through the artistry he brought to a medium whose results were confined to a small plate of glass but under the magic of illumination became part of nature sublime.

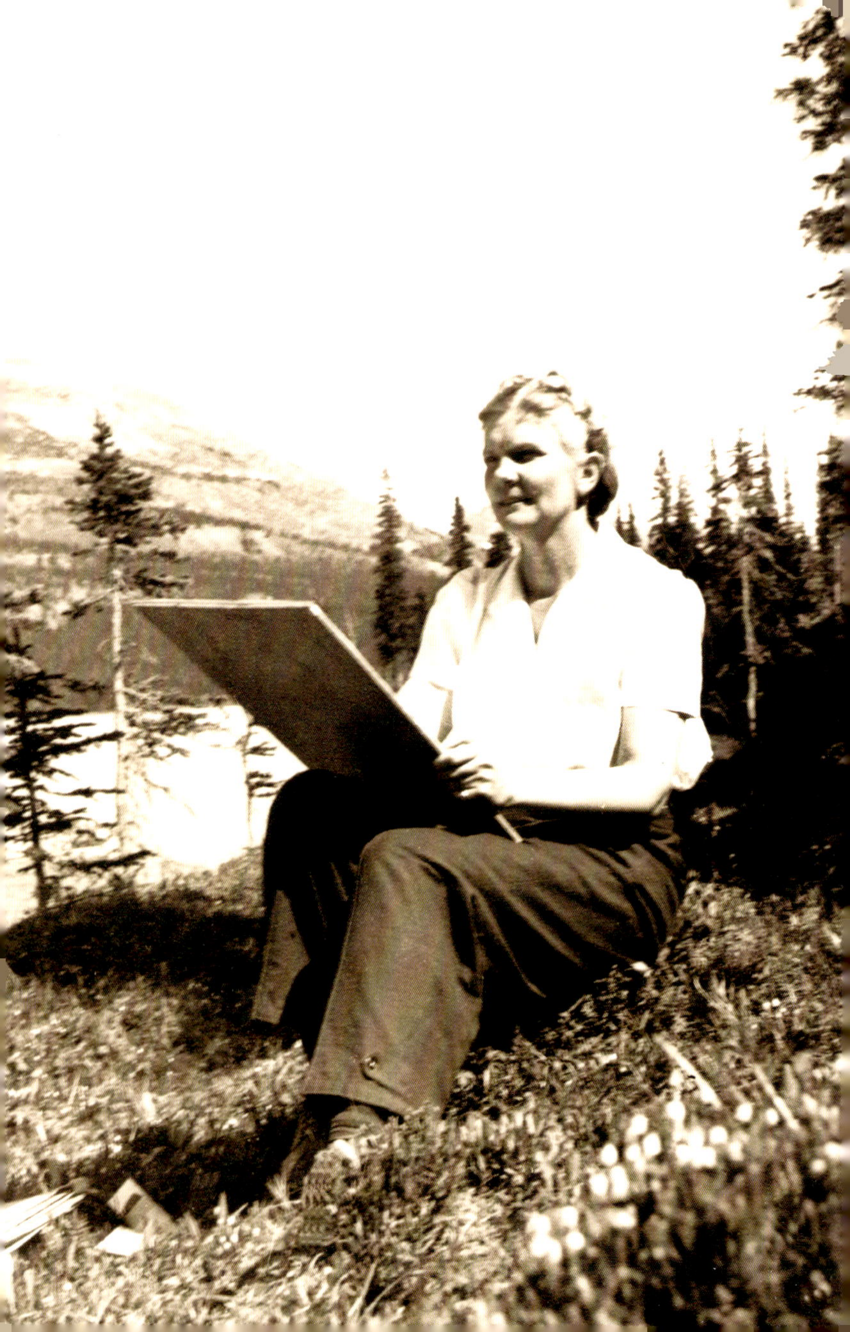

4

Annora Brown
(1899–1987)

Pick wildflowers? Assemble a collection of pressed plants? Not Annora Brown of Fort Macleod, Alberta. Neither of those activities had any appeal for her. Nor did she feel any excitement about painting flowers as botanical specimens as Mary Schäffer Warren or Mary Vaux Walcott had done in their lovely watercolours and hand-coloured lantern slides. Still, Brown's devotion to "Old Man's Garden" – as she referred to the local countryside – had made her into something of a local legend, an eccentric with a passion for painting the native perennials in her own style. Not all Albertans found Brown's fascination with the local flora a subject worth painting, however. She remembers a friend saying, "Too bad you have to stay in this place. Too bad you can't go to England or France. There you would really find something to paint."[36]

As a young girl at the turn of the previous century, Brown had indeed picked and pressed, aided by her mother as they searched for names in old copies of Gray's and Spotton's botanies. Alas, many of the plants cited were not found in their own untamed and spacious "backyard." In fact, as far as Annora Brown's own world was concerned, it was *terra incognita*, a place where the echo of the frontier still resonated and was considered by some to be deficient in all things "civilized." But, as this painter was to discover, the country she was beholden to enriched her in ways that no London or Paris ever could have.

I think I can understand the attraction Brown felt for this part of Canada. Located in the southwest corner of Alberta, it is an area I deeply love. I am enthralled with such places as Livingstone Gap, Head-Smashed-In Buffalo Jump, the incomparable drive through the historic ranchlands lining Highway 22 and the Whaleback, where a two-day hike through its undulating montane landscape with my mother, Irene, revealed a rich plethora of wildflowers and other native vegetation. It is a spectacular and varied place, with evocative names like Porcupine Hills, Devil's Peak, Jerry Potts Bottom, Chief Mountain and Belly Buttes. Many names are Blackfoot in origin and through Annora Brown's contacts with the nearby tribes of the Blood (Kainai) and Peigan (Piikani), she became inspired by their stories and knowledge of the locale.

As a second-generation inhabitant of windy Fort Macleod, Brown also knew about the community's own beginnings, the most celebrated being the site of the first North-West Mounted Police outpost in western Canada. When the post was established, on an island in the Oldman River in 1874, large herds of bison were still present, but by the time Brown was an infant the buffalo were already only a memory. The artist would have appreciated that no matter whether you were a native of a reserve, a resident of the town or a member of the NWMP – as Brown's English father, Edmund,* was from 1886 to 1895 – the Oldman was the most significant watercourse in the region.

This rocky-bottomed, shallow ribbon of the freshest kind, flowing roughly eastward from the Rocky Mountains, is named for the Blackfoot creator god and trickster Old Man, or Napi. A mythical being, this impulsive character appears in Brown's first book, *Old Man's Garden*, as the one who brings the territory into

* Edmund Forster Brown immigrated to Canada from London in 1885. After retiring from the police, he briefly returned to homesteading near Red Deer, where his daughter, Annora, was born in 1899.

existence. Of Old Man's contribution to the creation of abundance in the area, Annora Brown wrote:

> No puny efforts nor specializing in a few varieties in Old Man's Garden! He has flowers of the open prairie of course, and flowers of the moist dark forests, flowers that grow at low altitudes … and flowers that cling to dizzy mountain heights … [but perhaps] his Rock Garden is the greatest of his undertakings … he has given us the unique possession of a garden where one may climb from summer back to spring and even to the very edge of winter in the short space of a single hour.[37]

First published in 1954, *Old Man's Garden* is very unlike the earlier guidebooks by Mary Schäffer and Stewardson Brown, Mary Vaux and William Copeland McCalla. Literary historian George Melnyk[38] has compared *Old Man's Garden* to the much earlier, and better known, *Canadian Wild Flowers*, by Ontario's Catherine Parr Traill. While concerned with the region's native plants, including their botanical characteristics, Brown's writing and black and white illustrations create an even larger picture of the milieu these plants inhabit, by incorporating the stories and anecdotes of First Nations people, early settlers and ranchers and the accounts of early European explorers. Written from this unusual perspective, the book also serves as a chronicle of western Canada. And, while by today's standards some of Brown's prose can seem overly romantic in tone and racially insensitive, *Old Man's Garden* is – in the postmodern lingo of today – a "multi-layered" narrative where many voices participate in its telling.

It's also a book bursting with personality and a deep sense of place that could only be conveyed by someone with Brown's roots and connections. Just a few years after its publication, the Calgary Exhibition & Stampede Salon of Fine Arts released exhibition publicity crediting Brown with proposing that wildflowers are as much a part of the western heritage as "Indians and cowboys."[39] To make her point, among the cowboy bronzes and ranch-themed paintings at the 1961 Stampede, Brown displayed nine works, most of them dealing with the floral richness found beneath the feet of every westerner who cares to look.

If Annora Brown was a second-generation inhabitant of Fort Macleod, she was also, to a wider degree, a first-generation pioneer of an emerging artistic community in Alberta. Prior to the 1930s there were few avenues available for artistic training in the West. So, as also experienced by others of her generation, her introduction to the world at large and its cultures began at home and in her community.

In Brown's case, much credit must go to the Fortnightly Club, formed in 1908 with the motto "Let every woman be occupied in the highest ways of which her nature is capable."[40] Organized to study different countries in depth, including their artistic heritage, this local study group relied on books loaned by McGill University's extension department from distant Montreal. Fortunately for the young Brown, the club's enthusiastic librarian was her mother, an Ontario-born Quaker named Elizabeth Ethel Cody. Brown recounts how the Fortnightly Club provided opportunity to learn about "eastern perspective, Fujiyama and wood-block prints"[41] when the topic was Japan. Italy brought Michelangelo, Raphael and Titian to her attention, while the art of England was about Constable, Turner, Whistler, the Pre-Raphaelites and Ruskin. France, though, was a different story. The Impressionists, referred to at the time as the "Mad Men of Paris," raised the group's eyebrows. According to Brown:

> Because I was young I could not attend, but my mother told me about it, repeating some of the witty remarks [made at a meeting]. Then, with a small smile and in a quiet voice, she added, "It is just possible that those

men known more about painting than we do." Neither of us had any prescience of the role they would play in my life, of how I would come to admire them, to study their methods, their philosophies, even their private lives, until their work became part of my life.[42]

Another group that made an impact on Brown was the Women's Christian Temperance Union, a "much misunderstood organization,"[43] as the artist called it. The WCTU, and its activism on behalf of women's rights as well as for temperance, instilled in Brown a belief that women could play many roles in society, even non-traditional ones such as the artist she aspired to be. The WCTU's work was supported by Annora's mother and friends, bringing to the Brown kitchen table such notable suffragettes as Famous Five* members Nellie McClung of Calgary, Louise McKinney of nearby Claresholm and Henrietta Muir Edwards of Fort Macleod. Described by Brown as "an artist of some distinction,"[44] Edwards gave the young artist her unused art supplies and a very special book:

A sheaf of watercolour paper, at a time when the cost of even one sheet was inhibiting, did much to

* The five Albertans who championed a big win for Canadian women's rights in 1929 also included Emily Murphy of Edmonton and Irene Parlby of Lacombe-Red Deer.

> release me from a cramped and timid style ... [and] a book on the wild flowers of eastern Canada written by Catherine Parr Traill, illustrated beautifully by her niece, Agnes Fitzgibbon, and published in Canada in 1869.[45]

From 1925 to 1929, Annora Brown finally obtained the professional art training she so desired, at the Ontario College of Art in Toronto. It was a vibrant time to be at the college, with instruction from such outstanding Canadian artists as George A. Reid, C.W. Jeffreys and Group of Seven members Arthur Lismer, J.E.H. MacDonald and A.Y. Jackson. Brown excelled in her courses, receiving scholarships and awards before graduating with a Diploma in Applied Design (Honours). Of the instructors who left the deepest impression on her, artistically and philosophically, the opinionated Arthur Lismer – in baggy suits of Harris tweed – had no rival. On his advice, and throughout her life, she filled dozens of sketchbooks with quick drawings and scribbled comments about everything she observed. From these renderings emerged her wildflower art, western landscapes and depictions of Blackfoot life and culture.

Lismer also had a way of putting into words the ineffable difference between what he, as an Ontarian, had long seen and described in his landscapes and what those who were from the Prairies saw. "If a fifty-dollar bill were lying at your feet, you westerners would not see it. You would be too busy looking at the distance,"[46] he once commented, in response to a lack of detail and description in the foreground of student sketches. Brown must have realized, as did many of her compatriots, that to make sense of anything west of the Canadian Shield, something different would be needed to capture the vastness of western land and sky.

Closer to the ground was her interest in wildflowers, which happily was reciprocated by her design instructor, the notable Robert Holmes. Preoccupied as an artist with the wildflowers of Ontario,* Holmes offered advice about the careful plotting of shapes and tones and allowing the areas of dark to "sing out" against the light. Stylistically this would become an enduring aspect of all of Annora's wildflower art. As the environmentally conscious Brown later recounted:

> We talked of wildflowers that had all but disappeared in Ontario, wiped out by the advancing hordes of humanity, and the myriad flowers of the West. My mind

* Wildflower watercolours by Robert Holmes (1861–1930) are found in the collections of the National Gallery of Canada and the Art Gallery of Ontario.

could not envisage a time, coming all too soon, when they too would be threatened.[47]

After graduating, Annora Brown returned to Alberta in 1929, having become, as she put it, "a new and unexpected self."[48] Now living in Calgary, she had art students to instruct at Mount Royal College, and on weekends there was new terrain for Brown and her artist friends to explore and sketch, such as the mountains around Banff. Closer to her hometown, the wildflower paradise of the Pincher Creek area, the Porcupine Hills and Waterton Lakes National Park also beckoned. Her friends included fellow westerners she had met at the Ontario College of Art – Illingworth Kerr and Euphemia McNaught – and as time went on, through the dire years of the Depression, when Brown returned to Fort Macleod to look after her ailing mother and then support her father and herself by painting and illustration, her circle widened to encompass many other artists who gave Alberta its first "visual" sense of itself. These included Marion and Jim Nicoll, Janet Mitchell, the indispensable Catharine and Peter Whyte and Walter J. Phillips.

When McNaught, Kerr and Brown had met at OCA, they were, in the context of Canadian art, the western

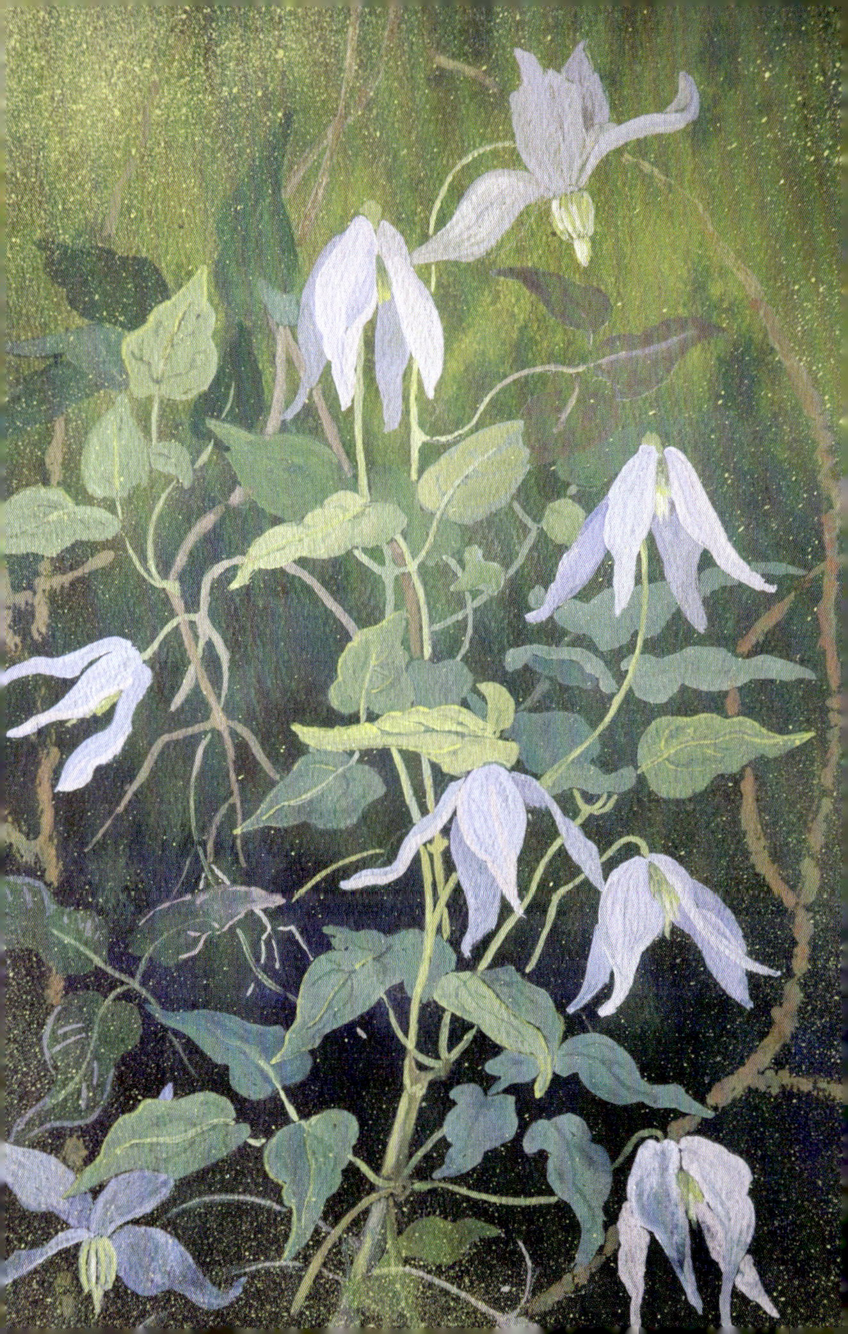

students who became aware of a "strange aberration"[49] which ironically to this day is not all that much different if one considers how many western names are absent from the Canadian canon:

> Canada, we discovered, consisted of Ontario, Quebec, Halifax and Peggy's Cove. There was an outpost called Winnipeg, which was known chiefly through the work of Walter J. Phillips, Lemoine Fitzgerald and Alexander Musgrove, and there was a narrow fringe of land along the Pacific, where the Indians raised totem poles in their villages. The country we had thought of as Canada was as little known as the Antarctic icecap.[50]

The West also seemed to be a "place" not especially valued by some who dwelled in the very heart of Napi country. If Brown's wildflower depictions were considered to be minor subject matter, an even greater puzzle, to the locals at least, were her oil on panel paintings of grain elevators, dust storms, native life and pioneer settlement. By the 1960s, attitudes would start to change, but even Brown could not forget being told by an observer during the Dirty Thirties that grain elevators were "ugly things"[51] to paint, and besides, nobody ever paints them. In that regard, "[Brown's] art must have been considered radical in rural Alberta of the 1930s,"[52] comments Patricia

Alderson, a scholar on Annora Brown. In a broader context, the artist was by no means alone; throughout North America, regional topics inspired many artists of her generation. Also, Arthur Lismer's advice to "capture the abstract quality inherent in the landscape rather than simply paint an accurate rendition..."[53] made for a more colourful, more modern style, which suited Brown well but was still jarring to those around her who had no idea of more recent developments in European art.

This style applied equally to her wildflower art, as the botanical art tradition so fundamental to the watercolours of Mary Schäffer and Mary Vaux played no role in Brown's own oeuvre. Firmly located in an evolving Canadian art tradition, a student of the Group of Seven, she practised in an idiom that belonged more to the (early) 20th century than the 19th. Wildflowers were the one subject that sold well for her as a professional artist, and Brown once estimated that it accounted for about half of her artistic output. In the 1930s, she sold small-scale watercolours, typically about five by three inches, with a bright flower rendered against a dark background, for a dollar apiece. (Brown recognized these small, quickly done pieces were a means of survival during the Depression and later admitted they were not always her best work.)

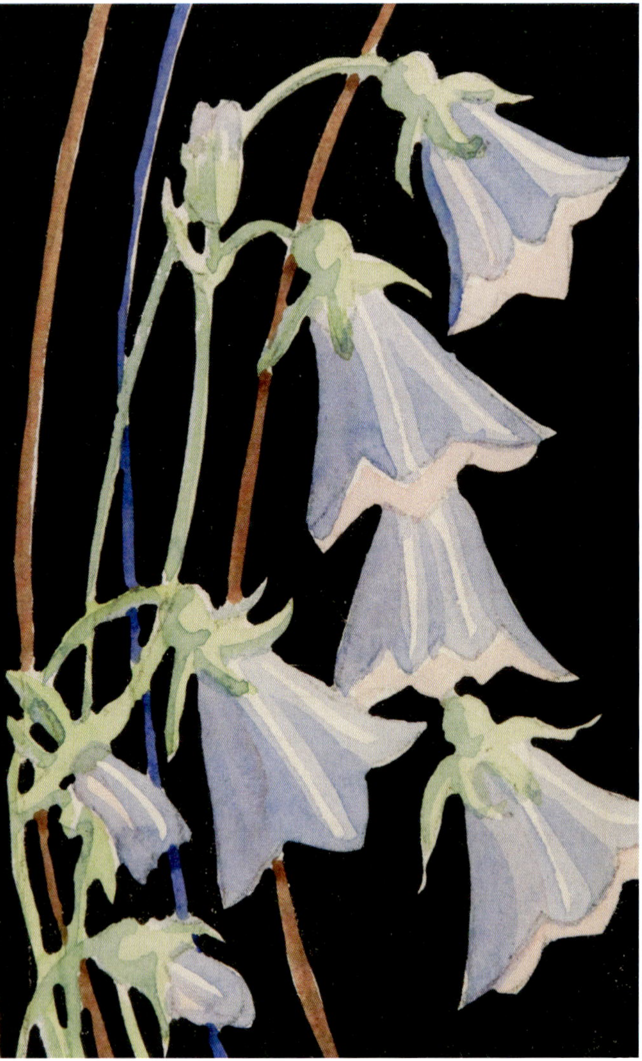

She also designed stencils for needlework and hooked rugs in response to the enormous popularity of handicrafts in a time when people had only nickels and dimes for anything creative. Her wildflower art and landscapes populated with native perennials made their way into the annual exhibitions she submitted to, for example, the Alberta Society of Artists, Calgary's post-war Coste House (Calgary Allied Arts Council), Calgary Sketch Club and, farther afield, the Art Association of Montreal, National Gallery of Canada and Canadian Society of Painters in Watercolour.

A poignant photograph from 1950 shows the middle-aged artist standing in her backyard with her arm around her elderly father. In the foreground and background is a large wildflower garden cultivated with plants brought home from her sketching trips. Apparently, Brown managed to grow over a hundred species, a living "library" that no doubt was important in the writing of *Old Man's Garden* and possibly in the execution of two hundred watercolours for Calgary's nascent Glenbow Foundation.

The latter project, begun in 1958 on a commission for the museum's collection, resulted in a body of wildflower work that presented another side of Brown's artistic personality. It took her three years to complete the series,

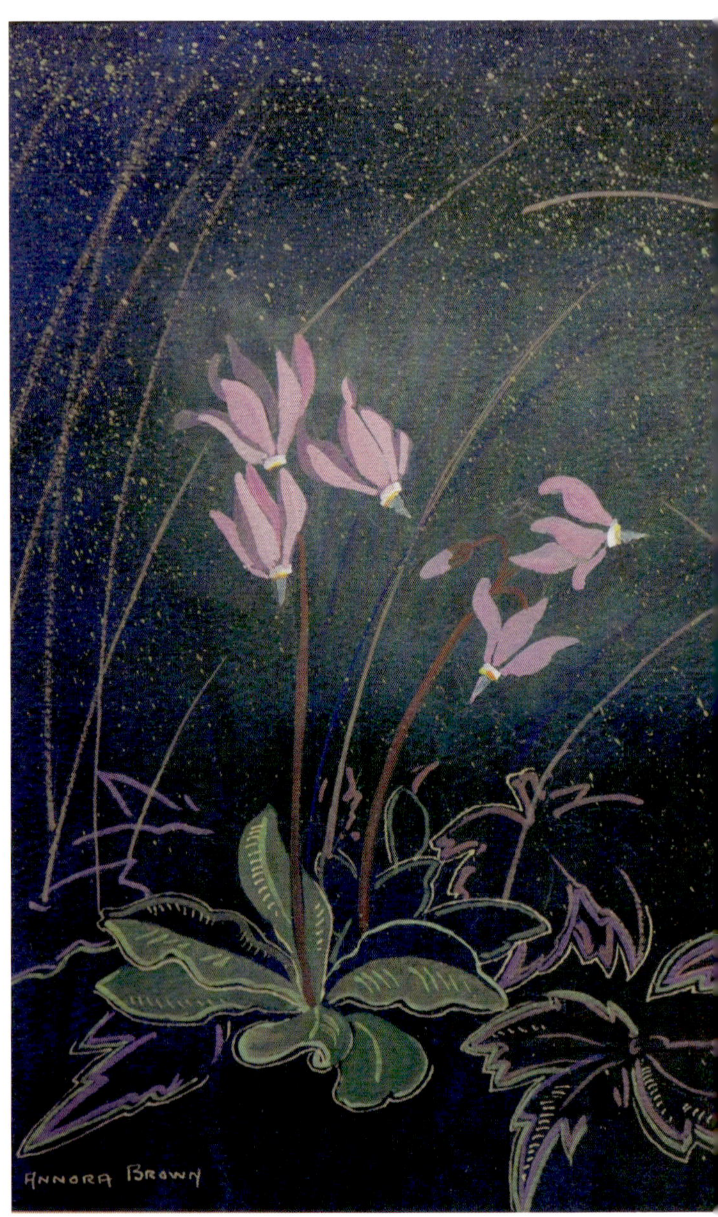

Shooting Star

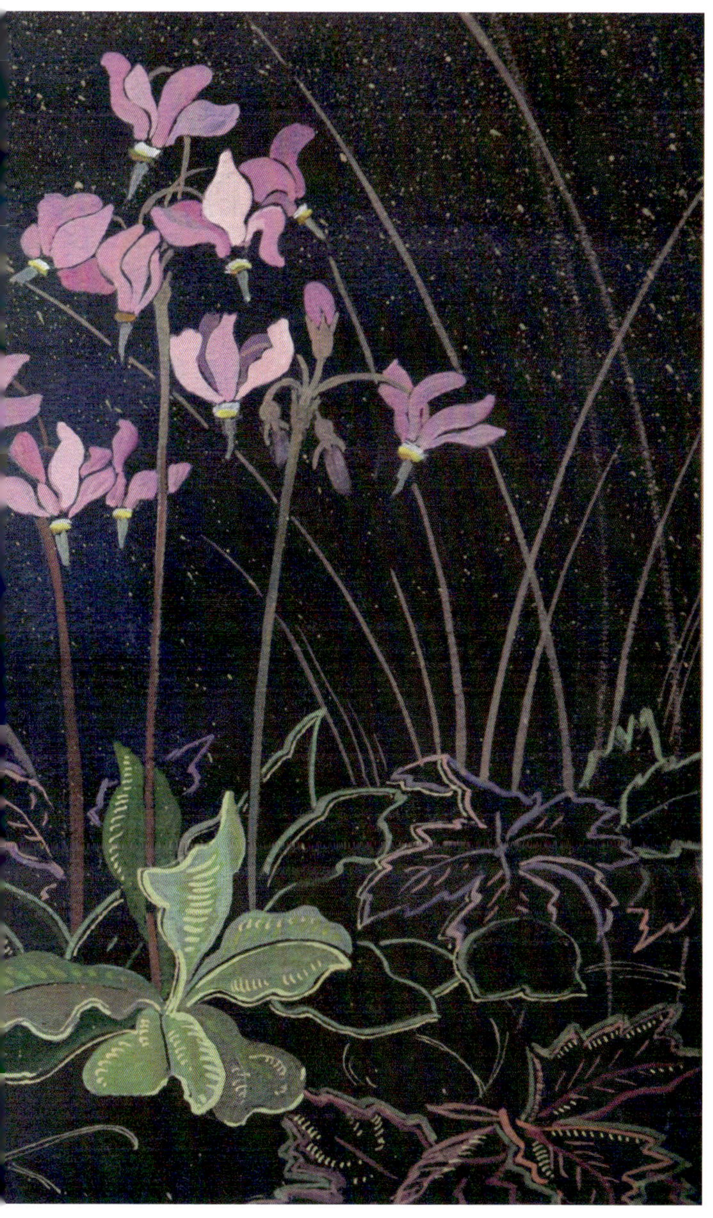

and when she did, the number of watercolours was closer to five hundred, as many were purchased individually by admirers as fast as she completed them. Two hundred of these works now reside in the Glenbow Museum collection, with still more in private collections. *Shooting Star* and another watercolour titled *Twin Flower & Canada Dogwood* belonged to historian and writer Eleanor Luxton, of Banff's enterprising Luxton family.* Both were painted with the addition of casein – a milk-like substance which adds an opaque quality to certain areas of the picture, such as the flower petals. Despite their small size, these enhanced flowers have a more distinct presence and almost glow in their darkened surroundings. Not all the flowers and their foliage are filled-in with pigment though. Some are only outlined in crisp, opaque colour, which suggested to Patricia Alderson that they represent "the spirit of flowers past or perhaps yet to come."[54]

In keeping with Brown's desire to depict native plants in their surroundings, these paintings do give some indication of places where these plants are found. Still, the environment they inhabit in the work seems more intimate and imagined than based on an actual location.

* These watercolours are in the collection of The Eleanor Luxton Historical Foundation, Banff.

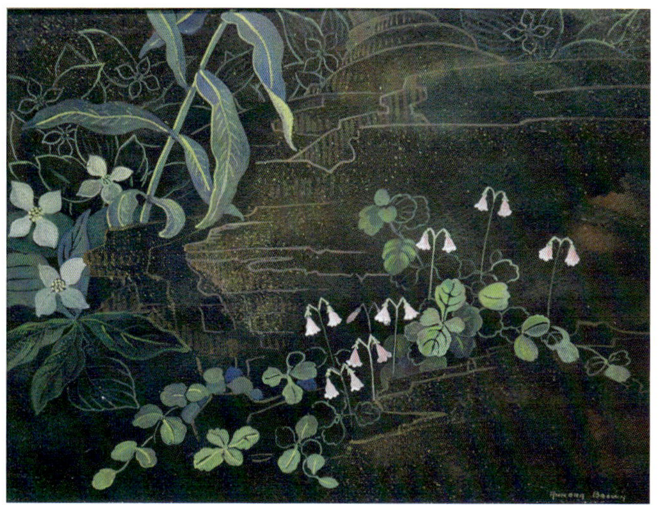

Twin Flower & Canada Dogwood

Nonetheless, the flowers depicted have movement and are an eminent presence in the natural world. Many of these watercolours are finished with starry flecks of light-coloured paint, and, as a whole, these images seem to beckon back to the artist's childhood when she once examined a blackeyed susan up close: "I suddenly felt a presence all around me, as if the spirits of the earth had come out to share a moment with me."[55] It is that moment, perhaps, which Annora Brown conveys many years later in these delicate and whimsical portrayals.

In addition to this significant body of work, Brown's interpretative skills also took her in more boldly stated

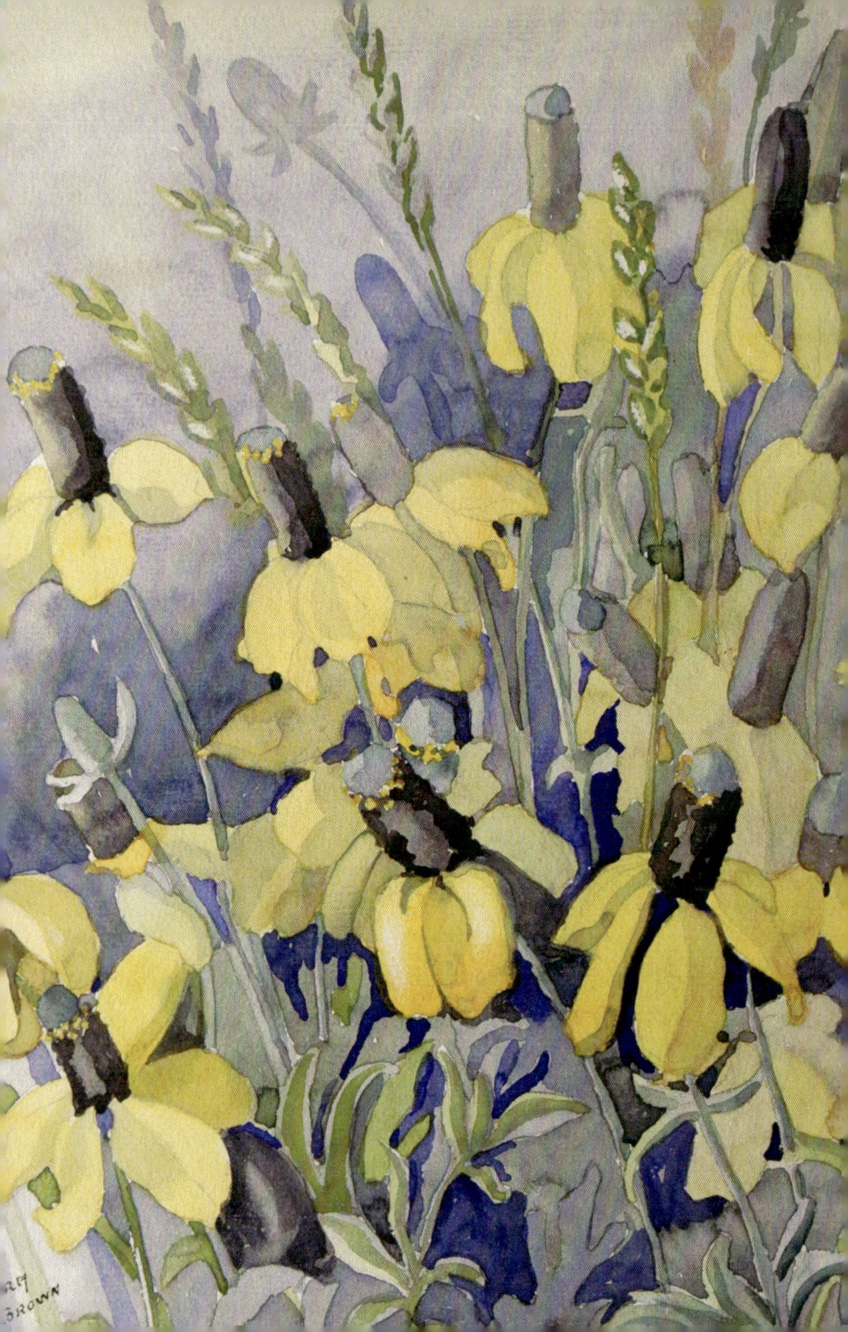

directions, underlined by a less controlled application of paint. *Coneflower*, *Wild Rose* and *Rosehip* are striking for their spontaneity and appearance as larger-than-life characters. Regarding the coneflower, Brown noted:

> It is even more decorative than the thistle but has not yet become well enough known to compete with it. With its drooping rays and purple-black cylindrical centre, a cluster of these flowers is like a troupe of gold dust twins, with stiffly starched yellow skirts outspread and little black bodies, ready to step in a summertime masque.[56]

As for the wild rose and its rosehip, she places this deciduous shrub in a larger context, writing that in the knowledgeable opinion of "[the] agricultural departments of the western provinces ... roses are weeds"[57] in need of eradication, with advice to farmers that they "plough [the shrub under and] fairly deep using a sharp share." That was the opinion of the experts, but Brown was not so sure about its usefulness. In *Old Man's Garden*, she recounts the experience of Daniel Harmon of the fur-trading North West Company, where the rose "was neither a weed nor the fondest child of dimpled Spring. It was a grim necessity." Harmon recalled how he and his

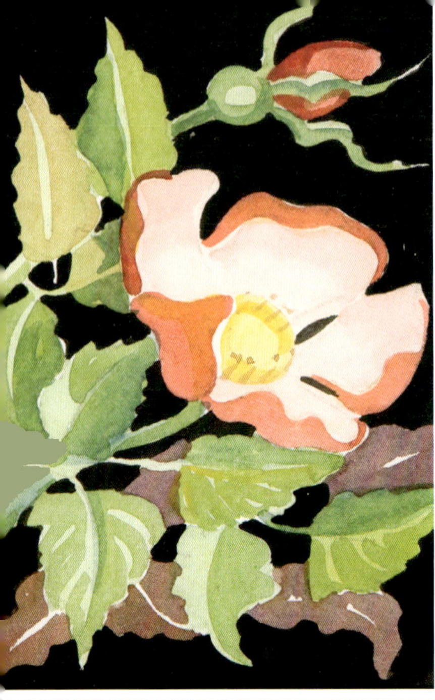

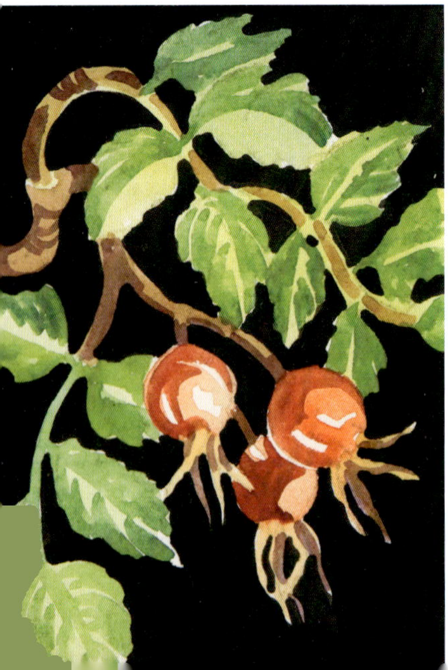

fellow fur traders passed the winter subsisting on rose buds: "... a kind of food neither very palatable nor very nourishing, which we gathered in the fields. They were better than nothing, since they would just support life."

It's tempting to wonder if the small-scale *Wild Rose* and *Rosehip*, with their black backgrounds, are Depression-era works of the kind Brown sold for a dollar apiece. They are undated, as is much of her art, since she rarely made note of when a painting was completed. This lack of regard for dates is also evident in her 1981 autobiography, *Sketches from*

Wild Rose

Rosehip

Life. As to the reason why she would prefer it this way, she wrote in what is thought to be a later note: "Dates, like railway guides, are enormously useful in their proper place. But an artist's autobiography tells about a pilgrimage of the mind and heart. There are no railway guides to the mystical land of the spirit."[58]

By the time her autobiography was published, Annora Brown was a retiree living on Canada's West Coast, and in that pilgrimage, which was to end with her death from breast cancer in 1989, she had, as Patricia Alderson put it, "ventured to find the identity of her region within itself, as opposed to its relationship with other parts of the country (Alderson)."[59] What was so different about what she found and conveyed so beautifully through her oeuvre were the floral denizens of Napi's garden. Painted in watercolour but also in words, she strove to give them a place where they were more than just a fine visual feast in a vase or a botanical specimen for a flower press.

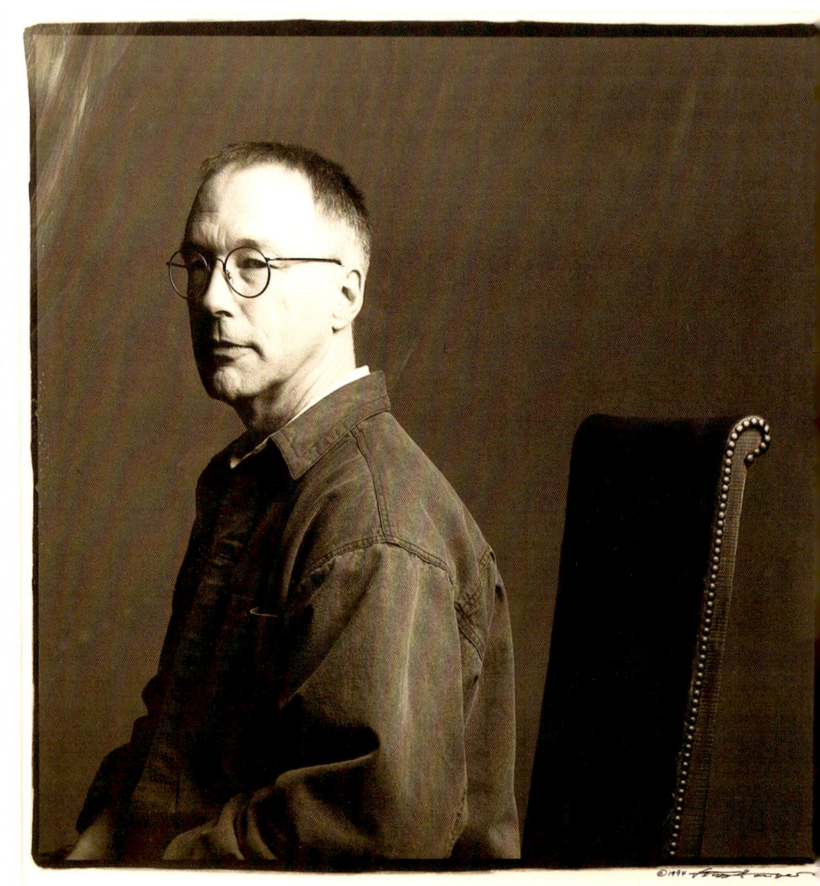
©1994

5

Robert Sinclair

(1939–)

At their smallest and most intimate, Robert Sinclair's watercolours are no more than six inches square. As featured in this book, his tiny wildflowers may indeed be the most delicate and fairest of them all, rendered by a male artist who remembers, as a youth, how his interest in the subject of flowers struck some people as "odd." Suitable for a woman, perhaps, like painter Georgia O'Keeffe (1887–1986), who is now celebrated for her abstract interpretations of that most "feminine" of themes.

But when the Edmonton artist's floral fascination surfaced, with watercolours of the showy amaryllis and other domesticated flora, it was his landscape art that was attracting all the critical attention. That was in the 1970s, when his spare, semi-abstract paintings of rolling foothills

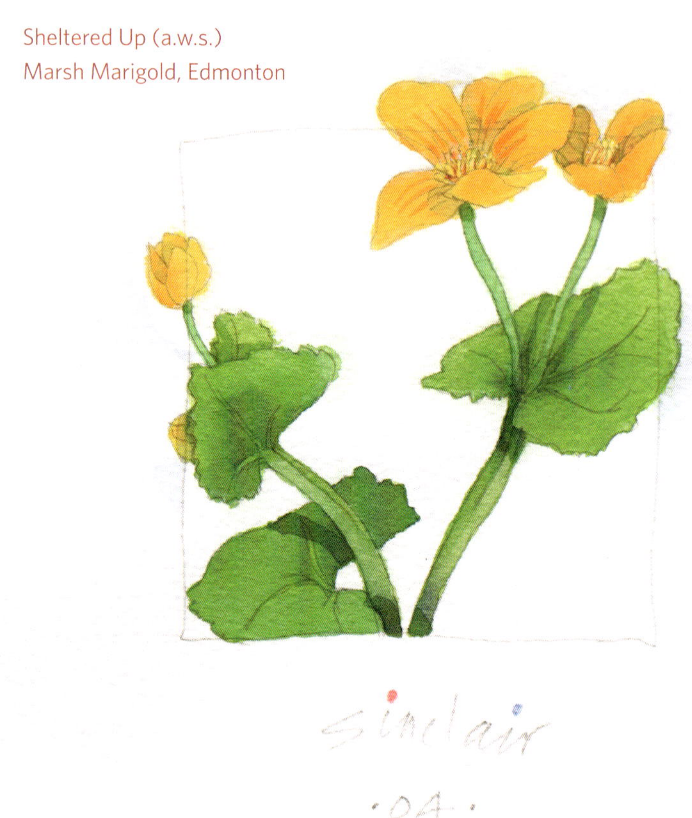

Sheltered Up (a.w.s.)
Marsh Marigold, Edmonton

and alpine terrain had audiences – from Edmonton to Toronto – lined up out the gallery door. For a serious painter with aesthetic roots in abstract painting, was the addition of the floral theme a risky move, considering it is a minor subject in the Western art tradition? Nearly forty years later, Sinclair's answer to this query was to send me a poem in which he suggests:

> the power of the flower is much underestimated in
> today's world
> ... but the flower smiles
> ... and is not concerned
> ... as it is always here
> ... as it has always been
> ... for no other reason than its own
> ... and for this
> ... we should respect such wisdom.[60]

"They don't need us,"[61] Sinclair emphasized to me later, smiling at the thought, and guided, as he often is, by his immersion in Eastern philosophy.

All of Sinclair's miniature portraits of wildflowers are titled with the abbreviation (a.w.s), for Alberta Wildflower Series (see below at p. 116). Of the four represented in this book, two examples are *Sheltered Up (a.w.s) Marsh Marigold, Edmonton* and *Youth Open (a.w.s) Wood Lily, Jasper*. Both species are framed within a drawn square, suggesting a window into their world. But, rather than waiting to be admired, both his lily and his marigold* seem on the verge of bursting out of their confined space.

* The plant is not a true marigold, but a member of the Buttercup family.

Youth Open (a.w.s.)
Wood Lily, Jasper

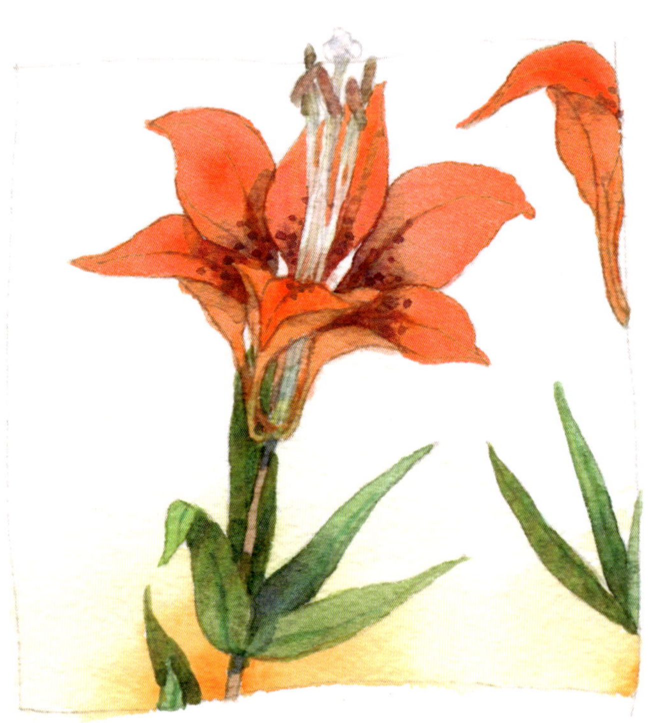

With an understated delicacy, their organic form is realized through a finely executed sketch and subtle shifts in applied watercolour. As with the work of Annora Brown, Sinclair's botanicals are drawn from observation but still painted from memory. "I want to somehow transcend the flower's description ... to put down [on paper] their aliveness, their spirit."[62] Or, as one art critic described it, "[Sinclair] lets the actors in nature's garden 'play' step to the front of the stage."[63]

Sinclair also sees flowers, whether domesticated or wild, as "highly sexualized beings,"[64] a concept not difficult to understand when one considers that the flower is in fact the plant's sexual organ. And while the petal tips of the marsh marigold may have the remarkable ability to attract insects by reflecting ultraviolet light, nothing quite compares to that highly prized family of plants the *Orchidaceae*. Orchids were associated with fertility by the ancient Greeks, and by some estimates they are the largest family among the world's flowers. It was the shape of the plant's tuberous roots which gave the plant its Greek name, *orchis*, or testicle. More recently, "Gorgeous Testicles – Beautiful Orchids"[65] was the witty phrase used by a popular mountain guidebook to describe the subject.

But more attractive to artists like Sinclair is the plant's unusual pouch-shaped flower, which has no

Shy Salute (a.w.s.)
Yellow Lady's Slipper,
Edmonton

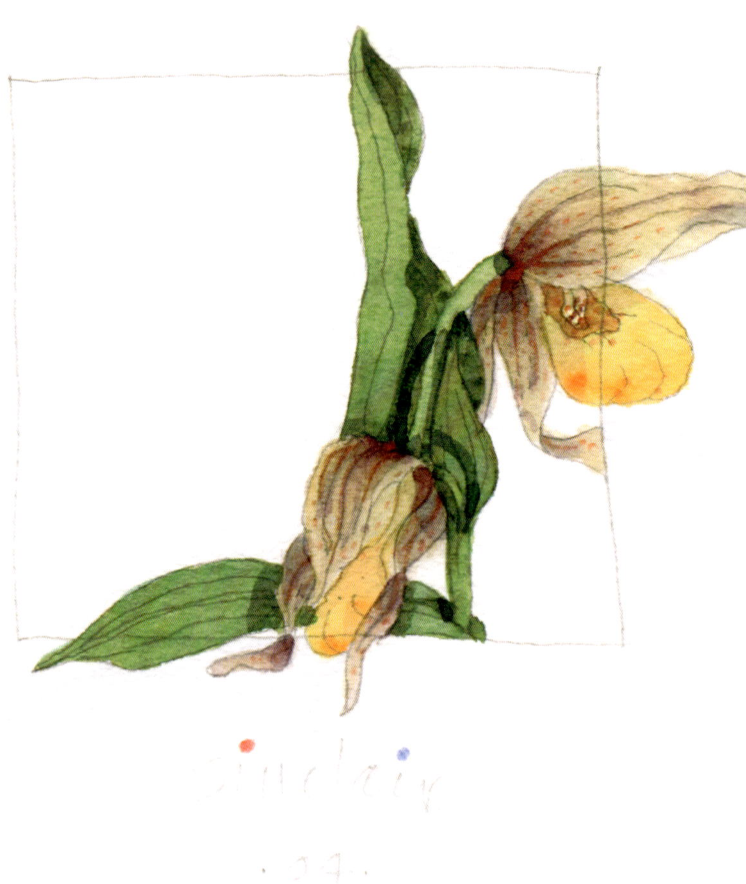

other purpose than to entice pollinating insects. In one of Sinclair's watercolours depicting a pair of Yellow Lady's Slippers, the one to the right, with its protruding pouch, waits eagerly for its next admirer. Once that insect is inside, there will be no exit without first being covered in pollen. Noticeably, the other flower is nowhere near as accessible. Its demeanour is entirely different – drooping, as it does, at the bottom of the image, veiled or enclosed by its brownish sepal.* Is this the individual behind the artwork's title: *Shy Salute (a.w.s) Yellow Lady's Slipper, Edmonton*?

There are four species of *Cypripedium*, or lady's slipper, in Alberta and the Rocky Mountains, with the yellow variety being the best known and most widespread. In early summer, along a wide strip of powerlines near where I live in Canmore, this elegant and charming plant can be found in impressive numbers. So abundant, in fact, that it can be tempting to either pick or transplant some into one's own garden. As with most things that grow wild, though, there is always a catch to this kind of petal-pilfering. In the case of this primitive plant, their roots need a special fungus to keep them alive. Pick the flower and the plant dies. Dig it up and chances are the transplantation will fail. Thus, in the words of the well-known

* The leaf that encases the bud.

Rockies naturalist Ben Gadd, "I bring my eye down to the flower, not the flower up to my eye."[66]

Guidebook author and photographer Neil L. Jennings is another hunter of today's wild flora, including those that flourish farther east of the mountains in Cypress Hills Provincial Park. Straddling the Alberta–Saskatchewan boundary, this rolling, tree-covered piece of paradise is the highest point in Canada between the Rockies and Labrador. According to Jennings, the Cypress Hills are said to "host the largest diversity of orchids of any place in the prairies."[67] The key word here is "diversity" and it's a condition extending to other plants in that region as well, such like the commonly seen Wild Rose.

On one visit to the park, Sinclair was intrigued by the sight of a rose shrub smothered in large blossoms – not pink, not red, but white. In other words, a native plant worthy of a watercolour, its festive blooms later celebrated in *Double Shot (a.w.s) Prairie White Wild Rose, Cypress Hills*. Belonging to the *Rosa woodsii* species, its flowers are described by Annora Brown as being even more beautiful than the "pink roses that clamber up the river banks in June."[68]

Brown does not identify the pink roses, but chances are they are *Rosa acicularis*, or prickly rose, also called the wild rose, the species that has served as Alberta's

Double Shot (a.w.s.)
Prairie White Wild Rose,
Cypress Hills

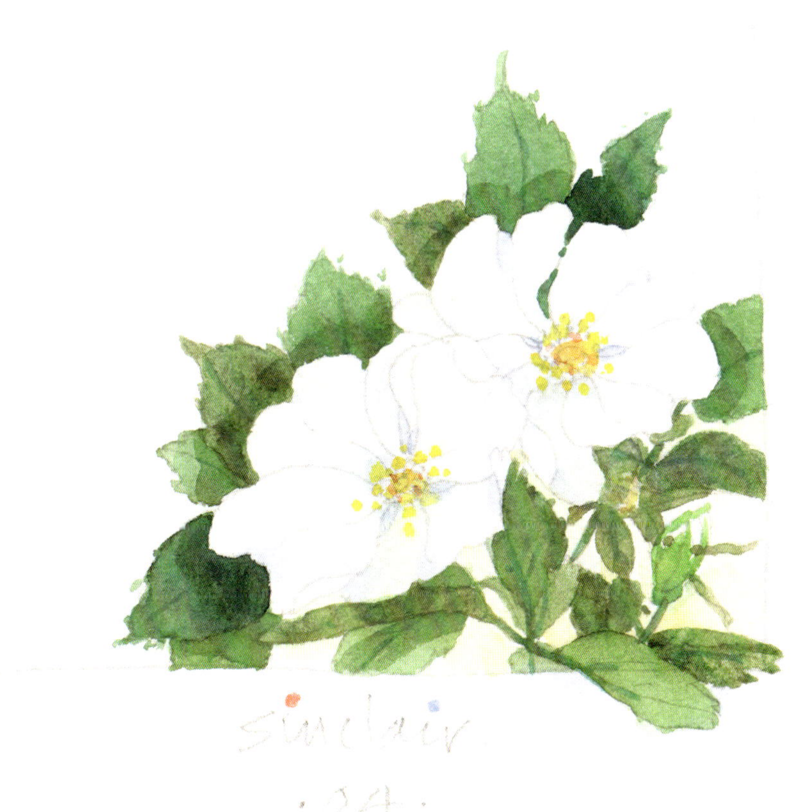

floral emblem for nearly eight decades. Sinclair has been inspired to portray this "patriotic" variety in several different works. In one instance, he made an embossed print where the surface of the paper is raised to emphasize the rose blossom's softly scalloped shape. Lightly touched with pink watercolour, this print owes its attractiveness not only to the embossed flower but also to its sturdy, one-of-a-kind paper. Employed for this artwork – as for all of Sinclair's watercolours – is Arches, a well-known art-paper stock from France that has an illustrious history dating back to the 15th century. Prized for its different grains and surfaces, this marvel of *papeterie* owes its existence not to the pulp of a tree but to that of the cotton flower. Made from what are called the linters, the youngest part of the flower, the pulp is known for its long, strong fibres. It seems, then, that from the image to the actual paper it is painted on, the theme of the flower reverberates again as it does many times over in Sinclair's artistic practice.

Another echo of the botanical lies in Sinclair's childhood. His mother was an avid gardener named Verita Florabelle Kittle. The name "Florabelle" seems almost too fitting to be true, but there it is, in the life of an artist whose growing years were spent on a prairie farm with his parents, Verita and Lorne Foster Sinclair. Born in

1939, in Saltcoats, Saskatchewan, Robert Sinclair holds a bachelor of fine arts from the University of Manitoba and a masters in fine arts from the University of Iowa. He has the distinction of being a native westerner who began his training at a western university and then found employment in the West as well,[69] at University of Alberta, where he taught art until 1997. When Sinclair was just starting out as a young instructor in 1965, his western pedigree was a relatively new phenomenon in Canadian art. It could only mean, as it did with others of his generation, that his response to the western environment might be something quite different from the past – the "past" as represented by the Group of Seven's prevailing portrayal of Canada as a place of northern lakes, romantic snow-covered French Canadian villages and, farther west, wild, inaccessible mountainscapes.

In Sinclair's landscape art, this meant composing, with a minimum of detail, paintings and sculptures where the landscape is pared away to a few simple elements: a lot of sky, a few hills or mountains, a flat stretch of land, and most notable of all, a two-lane road, its presence symbolizing not only the vast, empty space of the West but a different era, with a new perspective and a new identity. In addition, Sinclair playfully challenged the Group's dominance, with titles like the *Great Canadian*

Landscape for a series of hand-formed acrylic sculptures, and *Canada Classic* for a series of acrylic paintings on raw canvas.

Another challenge for the artist came with the idea of exploring a premise he had heard about in art school regarding the difficulty of painting with a lot of yellows and greens. To test this piece of aesthetic lore, Sinclair decided to use a calla lily from home and see how well he could deal with the greens of the plant's foliage. But the appeal of this exercise didn't last long. Instead, it was the composition of the plant itself, particularly the unfolding of the leaf and flower, that became the genesis of a new stream of drawing and painting. In other words, the telling of a life story using contemporary ideas like petals and stems only outlined, not filled in with detail or colour, and the use of cropping techniques or an off-centre focus.

Keenly motivated to somehow capture the sequence of stages in the flower's blooming, Sinclair set out to create, for instance, not a static image of an unfolding leaf as seen from one point of view but as seen from several perspectives. In one of his most intensive explorations of this theme, he produced 110 watercolours of an amaryllis from bud to bloom. A botanical tour de force, its clever sequential display on a very large wall enthralled audiences each time it was exhibited at the Edmonton Art Gallery (now called the Art Gallery of Alberta).* And, as unlikely a topic as plant life may be for an artist trained during the heyday of abstraction and other avant-garde movements, Sinclair always had enough contemporary content in how he handled this subject to keep most art critics in a positive frame of mind.

There were plenty of comments too about how this body of work was the most personal of Sinclair's oeuvre: contemplative and spiritually uplifting. As one curator explained, "The flower-plant pictures make no bows to regionalism, no glances over the shoulder to [Canadian] art history."[70] It was indeed art about something else, of botanical interest, yes, but not in its service.

Another aspect of Sinclair's engagement was his three-year study of oriental brush techniques, which complemented his already considerable drawing skills. In the blending of both eastern and western approaches, his fluid response to the floral world became distinctively his own, stamped, as it were, with his own signature. The result, as one admirer put it "are flowers at once powerful, delicate, tenacious and graceful."

Now in his 70s, Sinclair is an articulate and deeply thoughtful man who, through his teaching of tai chi, the

* The *Amaryllis Suite* is now part of the institution's collection.

Taoist practice of exercise and Buddhist meditation, has come to the conclusion that the flowering of many plants "touches the psyche deeply and that's what I recognize about them after they are done."[71] The same thought also applies to his more recent ambitions of recording the wild flora he sees around him as he hikes and ventures into the different ecosystems of the western landscape. Now known as the Alberta Wildflower Series, or (a.w.s), as we have seen, this project only emerged serendipitously when an art proposal featuring a mountain theme was rejected on the basis of "what's Albertan about that?" Sinclair concluded, quite tongue in cheek, that if mountains were not "Albertan" enough, then maybe wildflowers would be a better choice.

The artist is glad the question was asked by government officials and is also grateful that an invitation to lead a workshop* in floral depiction introduced him to the wonders of Waterton Lakes National Park. Containing fifty-two per cent of all the wildflower species found in Alberta, this ecological gem of a place, because of its greater annual precipitation, proved to be the perfect location for Sinclair to begin his province-wide floral exploration. In the ten years since, he has produced more

* This workshop, hosted by Willock & Sax Gallery, was a catalyst for the Waterton Wildflower Festival, now an annual event held each June.

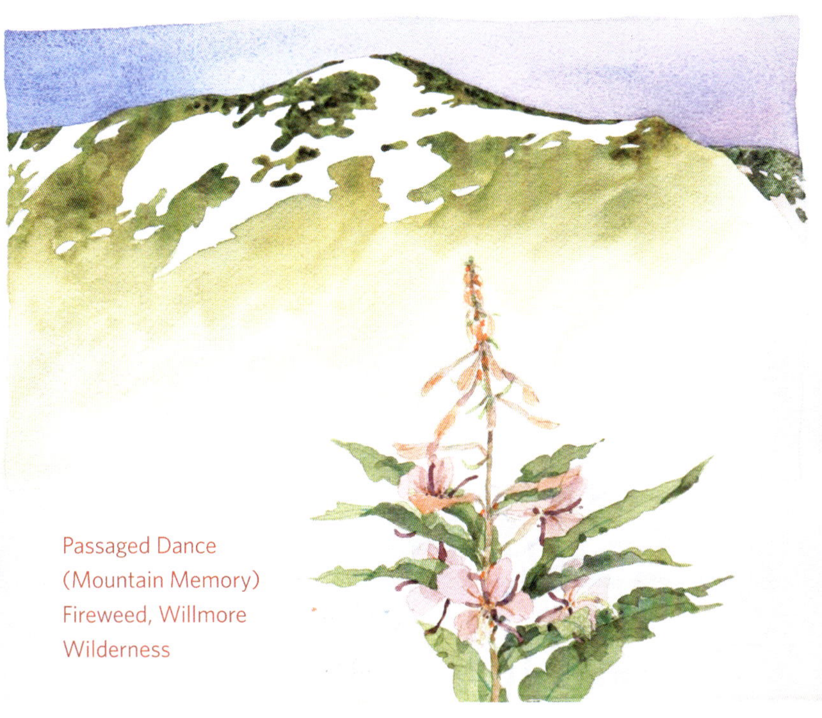

Passaged Dance (Mountain Memory) Fireweed, Willmore Wilderness

than four hundred watercolours, and many – certainly not all – of the flowering species have had their "moment" in miniature, on paper six inches square.

Sinclair has also worked with the wildflower theme on a larger scale, as with that late-summer showoff, fireweed, and the strong-smelling cow parsnip, the latter, surprisingly, part of the carrot family. Painted on 11 × 15-inch Arches, there is "a yin/yang dance happening," he writes, "as I balance the shapes with the ethereal gestures."[72] As always, and similar to his landscape art,

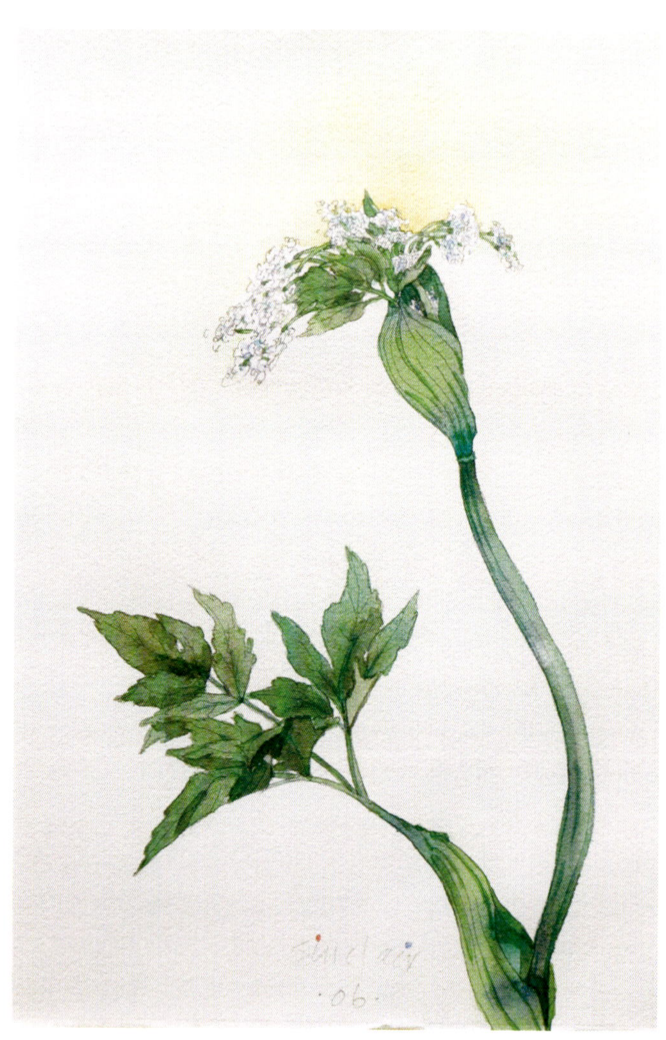

Flower Rain (a.w.s.) Cowparsnip

a quality of the understated and a lightness of touch prevails. In *Passaged Dance (Mountain Memory)*, *Fireweed, Willmore Wilderness* and *Flower Rain (a.w.s) Cowparsnip*, both perennials, common as they are, are indeed given their own "moment" as airy and exquisite folk seen along the trail or through the window of a passing car.

As with all of those fine women before him – Mary Schäffer Warren, Mary Vaux Walcott and Annora Brown – and that one exceedingly dedicated naturalist, William Copeland McCalla, Robert Sinclair's project asks us to remember the presence of the wildflower. More than simple decoration, more than a signpost of habitat, its appearance, whether in a wild locale or in a nearby urban park, is truly for the heart and soul. On a lighter note, as with the amaryllis, the calla lily and the begonia, the artist continues to highlight the fact that real men not only eat quiche, they enjoy flowers, too.[73]

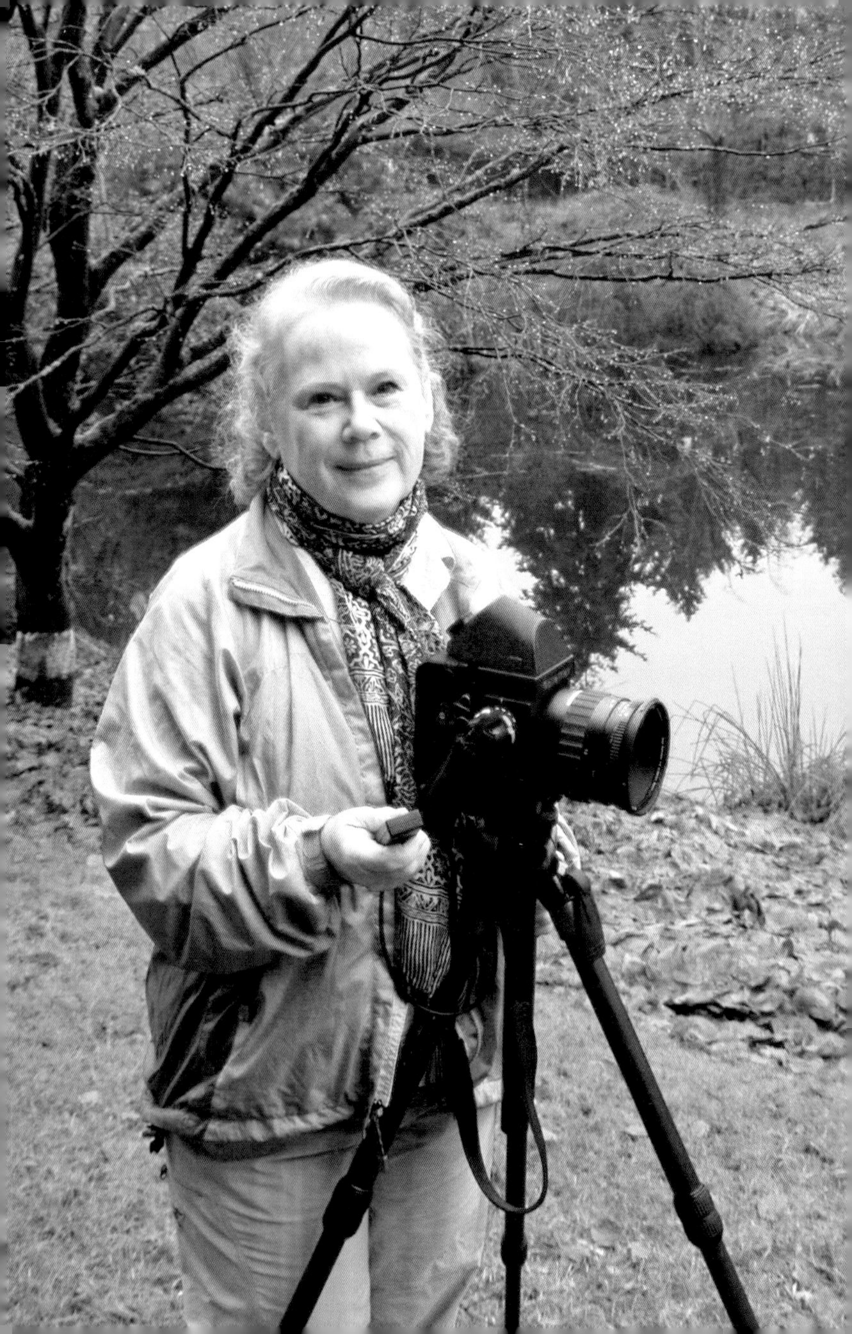

6

Carole Harmon

(1947–   )

Born in Banff, does Carole Harmon walk in the footsteps of those earlier women of mountain renown, Mary Schäffer Warren and Mary Vaux Walcott? In a way, yes, in search of flora to take her breath away. And if not quite that, then at least a few wild blue flax for her to photograph one miserable late spring day. A member of the geranium family, the single periwinkle-coloured blossom is one of the subjects of Harmon's *Windswept. Flowers and the Air Element.*

For a body of work about flowers and the bond they share with the wind, the photographer was partly inspired by novelist W.O. Mitchell's western Canadian classic *Who Has Seen the Wind?* The other flicker of inspiration came from the writing of US anthropologist Loren Eiseley. Harmon remembers how a 1957 Eiseley essay, "How Flowers Changed the World," set her to thinking about the wind "[being] a really pervasive element,"[74] playing a role in the spread of seeds, influencing how different flowers have evolved in different climatic conditions, and by extension having impact on human development as well. Wrote Eiseley:

> Without the gift of flowers and the infinite diversity of their fruits, man and bird, if they had continued to exist at all, would be today unrecognizable. Archeopteryx, the lizard-bird, might still be snapping at beetles on a sequoia limb; man might still be a nocturnal insectivore gnawing a roach in the dark. The weight of a petal has changed the face of our world and made it ours.[75]

Open to the prairie environment so sensitively recalled in Mitchell's novel, the artist took her camera to the windier and flatter terrain east of the Rockies. In the badlands of Alberta's Dinosaur Provincial Park and in the dry grasslands and rippled coulees in the vicinity of the Red Deer River, the wind indeed became Harmon's constant companion. Expressed in subtle and sometimes more dramatic ways, in the motion discernible in her photographs *Milk Vetch in Dinosaur Park*, *Old Man's Whiskers* and the breeziest of them all, *Wild Blue Flax*.

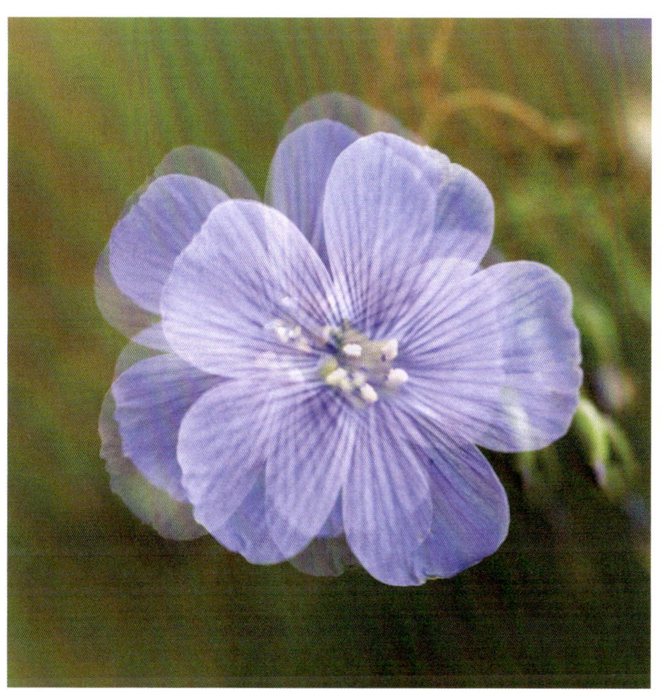

Wild Blue Flax

All three plants are denizens of the springtime, with the five-petalled flax, on the slenderest of stems, susceptible to the smallest of breezes. No wonder its genus name, *Linum*, is Latin for "flax" or "thread," cultivated since ancient times for the making of linen and cordage. And then there is that oddball, old man's whiskers,

Old Man's Whiskers (overleaf)

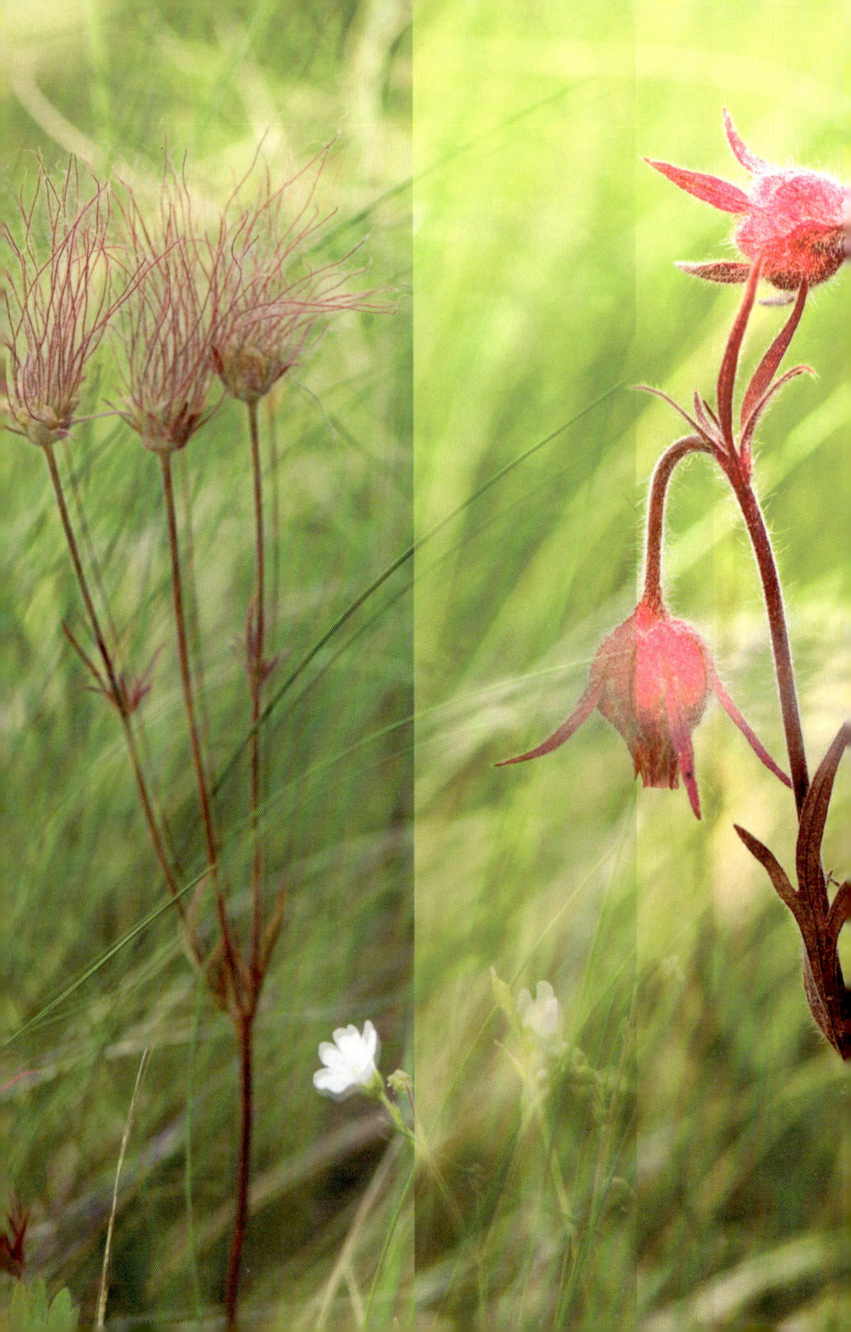

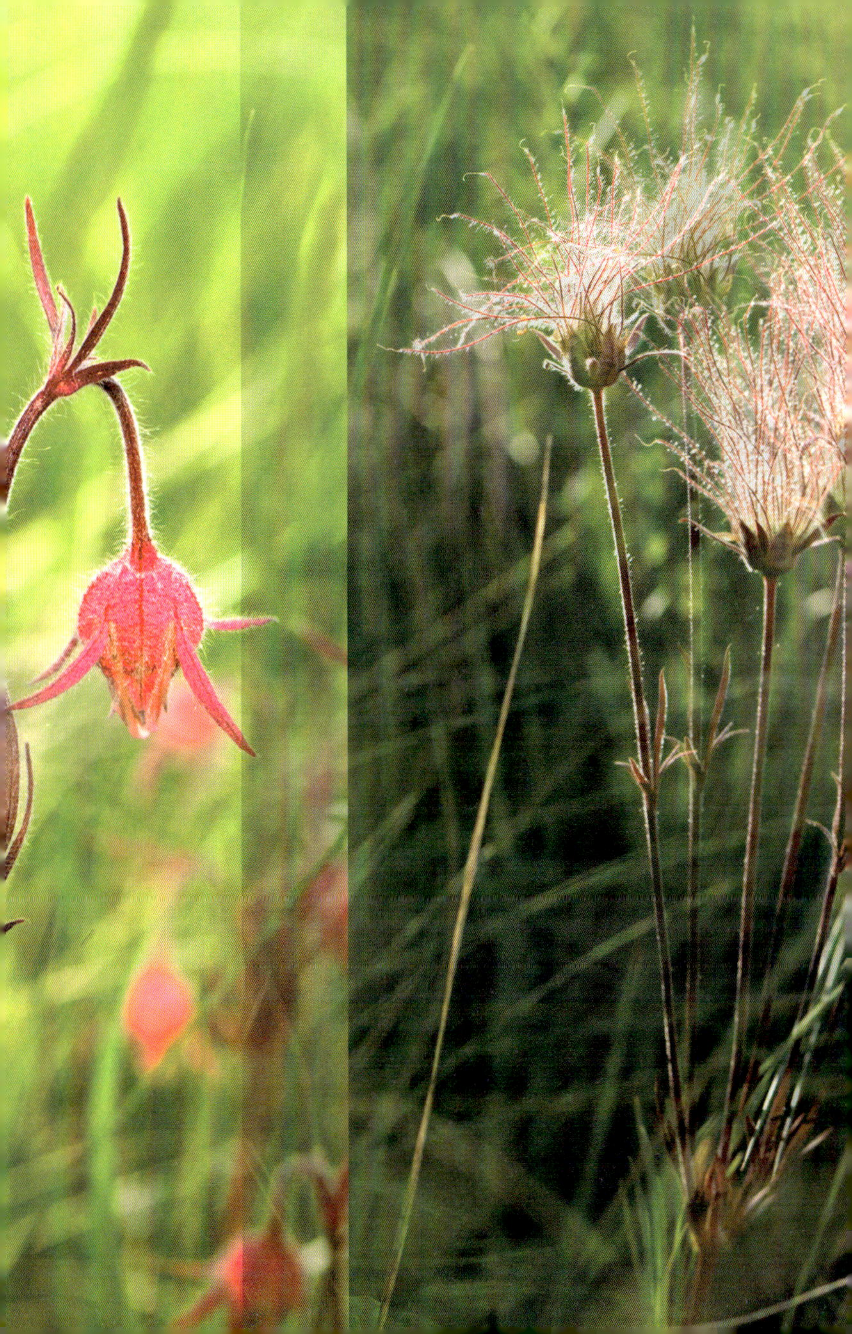

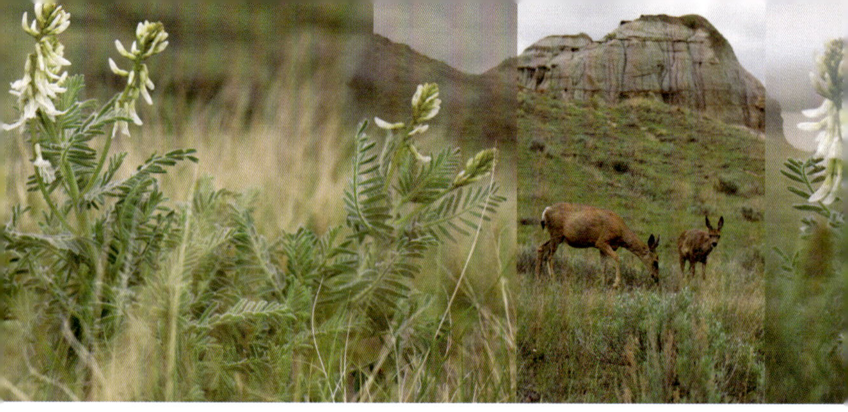

Milk Vetch in Dinosaur Park

or three-flowered avens as the perennial is sometimes called. It's the demurest of wildflowers, refusing to open fully when in bloom and producing a fruit of the most unexpected kind – a single, dry, single-seeded fruit attached to a feathery style* resembling a whisker. The real magic, though, begins when the fruit seed is distributed freely by the wind. If enough of them are around, the effect is like watching wisps of smoke blow across the prairie, hence its other common name, prairie smoke.

As for *Milk Vetch in Dinosaur Park*, it was at the end of the day when a doe and its fawn appeared in a field of pale-coloured vetch. Like Annora Brown, or at times Robert Sinclair, Harmon is engaged with the idea of portraying her subjects in the context where they appear.

* The slender stalk connecting the stigma to the ovary in the flower's female reproductive organ.

With an impressively eroded and rugged landform looming behind, the work conveys about this fossil-laden landscape a sense of the ancient past and the present. In this photograph and in *Old Man's Whiskers*, more than one state of time is being expressed through the combining or layering of several images. In the latter image, the three nodding flowers are flanked on both sides by the plant in a later stage of growth, fully in fruit but also rich in allusion to the whiskers of, well, an old man.

Where past and present meld or where, as Harmon writes, "formal elements and whimsical occurrences coincide," these are points of an "intersection," a characteristic she seeks to exploit in these compositions. Wildflowers lend themselves well to this approach because, as she explains, they are so transient: here today, gone tomorrow, their very ephemerality making the idea of time concrete.

Carole Harmon is acutely aware of how her approach to the "lowly" subject of the wildflower is very different from, say, what a Mary Vaux or a William Copeland McCalla achieved: a large, comprehensive visual record of what they encountered. Instead, working creatively at the start of a new century, Harmon is mindful of her own particular time and place. "Flowers and landscape are just considered pretty pictures," she told me. "So somehow I have to find ways to overcome that. I can put up the most beautiful picture of a flower and it will be invisible to people. I have to find some way of adding some other element that makes it more interesting." Not only that, while she still shoots some film whose images are scanned and then printed digitally, the photographer relies on the relatively new technology of shooting with a digital camera and loading those pictures directly into a computer, where multiple exposures and collages can be made with image-editing software. As a photographer, she works "cradle-to-grave," preferring to give the commercial photo labs a pass.

As for those who have walked (or hiked or ridden a horse) before her, the artist particularly admires Mary Vaux for her long engagement with a unique part of the environment that is less visible and known to others. She thinks Vaux's hefty, five-volume *North American Wild Flowers*, with its 400 vibrant watercolours, is "about the best it's going to get." In comparison, Harmon wouldn't even describe herself as an "amateur" botanist. That, she leaves up to others, including her aunt, Aileen Harmon, now in her late nineties, who worked for years as a naturalist with Parks Canada and was also an excellent photographer. Harmon remembers well a time when Banff was a different kind of community, with less development and nearby woods filled with flowers and wild strawberries. Somewhere in that past are recollections of crawling on the ground among this bounty and Aileen later introducing her, as a teenager, to the names of what she was seeing and admiring.

But if the earlier botanizing vocations of others like Vaux are one set of footsteps to consider, there is an even larger set, linked with the legacy of photography in the Canadian Rockies. Carole Harmon hails from two generations of pioneering mountain photographers: her grandfather Byron Harmon and her father, Don Harmon.* Both made their mark with substantial bodies of work that, in a sense, followed the development of photography in the 20th century, Byron as a black and white photographer labouring early in the century with 5 × 7 view camera and glass plates, and Don after the Second World War, on the cutting edge of mountain photography in colour. Together, their images made visual a largely untouched wilderness protected for its flora and fauna. In addition, their pictures of the mountain parks are not without historical interest: a majestic hotel near a sparkling alpine lake (Don Harmon) and a roped group of hikers along the top of a spectacular glacier (Byron Harmon) are just two

* Byron Harmon, (b. Olympia, Wash., 1876 – d. Banff, 1942); Don Harmon (b.1917, Banff – d. 1997, Banff)

examples. What is recorded is a golden era of mountain exploration, unknown landscapes and early tourism.

Of the two, Byron is the best known, often compared to the great US photographer Ansel Adams, whose pictures made Yosemite National Park a national icon. Wrote mountain scholar Robert Sandford:

> The moment it became possible to print black and white photographs cheaply, the world of seeing was utterly transformed. Byron Harmon was at the forefront of this movement. He explored and took more photographs of the mountain parks region than any other early photographer.[76]

Landscape is also where Carole Harmon began as a photographer, though not in the panoramic tradition. Instead, she was attracted to shooting things close up or in the middle range as she did with one of Canmore's Grassi Lakes in *Western Wood Lily*. More than a watery background, the clear, gem-green tarn is a liquid feast of chromatic intensity surrounding the ethereal, chalice-shaped lily. Harmon trained in black and white photography but found a monochromatic treatment was not enough for her exploration of the floral subject. Colour, for her, is about emotion, and with respect to her *Western Wood Lily*, the feeling evoked is one of reverence.

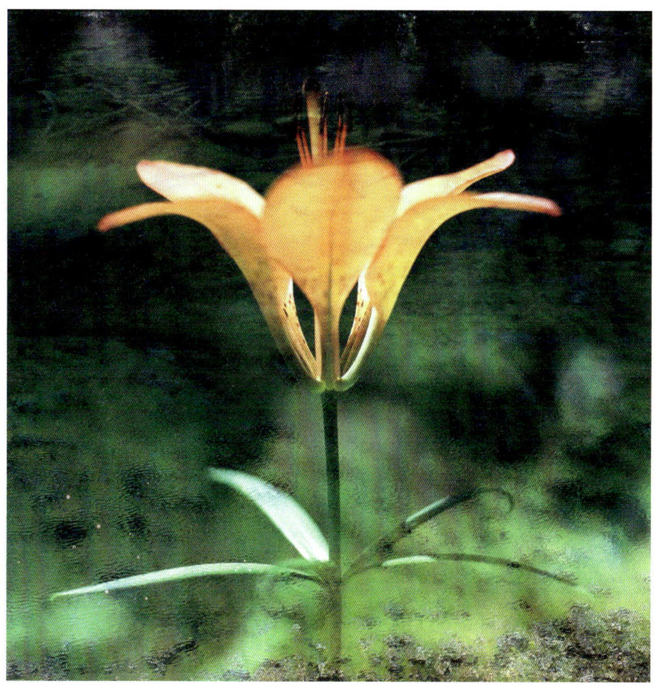

Western Wood Lily

With photography such a deep vein in the Harmon family, the expectation for a third-generation relative such as Carole Harmon might have been one of instant recognition. Not for her, though. She came to the medium almost accidentally when a cancelled trip to Europe to study mime led the bachelor of arts theatre graduate to enroll in a new photography program at the Banff School of

Fine Arts. There, under the instruction and enthusiastic energies of its new head, Bob Alexander, Harmon got the bug. Two years later, in 1973, she emerged conversant in many aspects of the photographic arts. But also awaiting her was a task requiring enormous commitment. On the heels of a Byron Harmon project initiated by fellow student Edward Cavell, and at the urging of Banff writer Jon Whyte, Harmon began to resurrect the faded reputation of her grandfather. Aware that his negatives* were stored in an old wooden filing cabinet in "rotting paper envelopes," the novice photographer, with the help of others, tackled Byron's collection of more than 6,000 images.

The results were stunning. There was an exhibition of Byron Harmon's photographs, *In Mountain Light*, which toured Canada and the United States, and a book, *Great Days in the Rockies: The Photographs of Byron Harmon, 1906–1934*, published by Oxford University Press and subsequently by Altitude Publishing.** Next would come a major book featuring Don Harmon's colour photographs, *Columbia Icefield: A Solitude of Ice*, containing

* Byron Harmon's original negatives are now in the collection of the Whyte Museum of the Canadian Rockies.

** Altitude Publishing Ltd. was launched in 1979 by Carole Harmon and Stephen Hutchings. It evolved into an important publisher of non-fiction books about the West.

pictures taken on two arduous packhorse journeys across the vast expanse of ice and snow. Carole joined her father on the second expedition, in 1975. By then, the camera had become her partner in representing nature through landscape and the depiction of its flora.

Carole Harmon's approach at the time of that remarkable trip was documentary, but as is inevitable with most artists, her definition of what she does with her subjects has changed a great deal. From straightforward recording, the presence of wildflowers and how they are handled in her oeuvre has widened and changed. Still comfortable with describing herself as a nature photographer who has also focused on other subjects, such as the neolithic standing stones of Brittany and the environment of Canada's West Coast, Harmon works on a project basis when pursuing what she calls "her ongoing love affair with wildflowers." Besides *Windswept: Flowers and the Air Element*, grasses and grass-like plants were the theme of *GRASS*, and the aftermath of a summer season marked by spectacular forest fires was revealed in a six-panel series, *Out of the Wildfire*.*

An artist Harmon especially identifies with is Annora Brown and her relationship with the environment. In

* This project was shown in its entirety as *Passing Through Fire* in Exposure 2008, Whyte Museum of the Canadian Rockies, Banff.

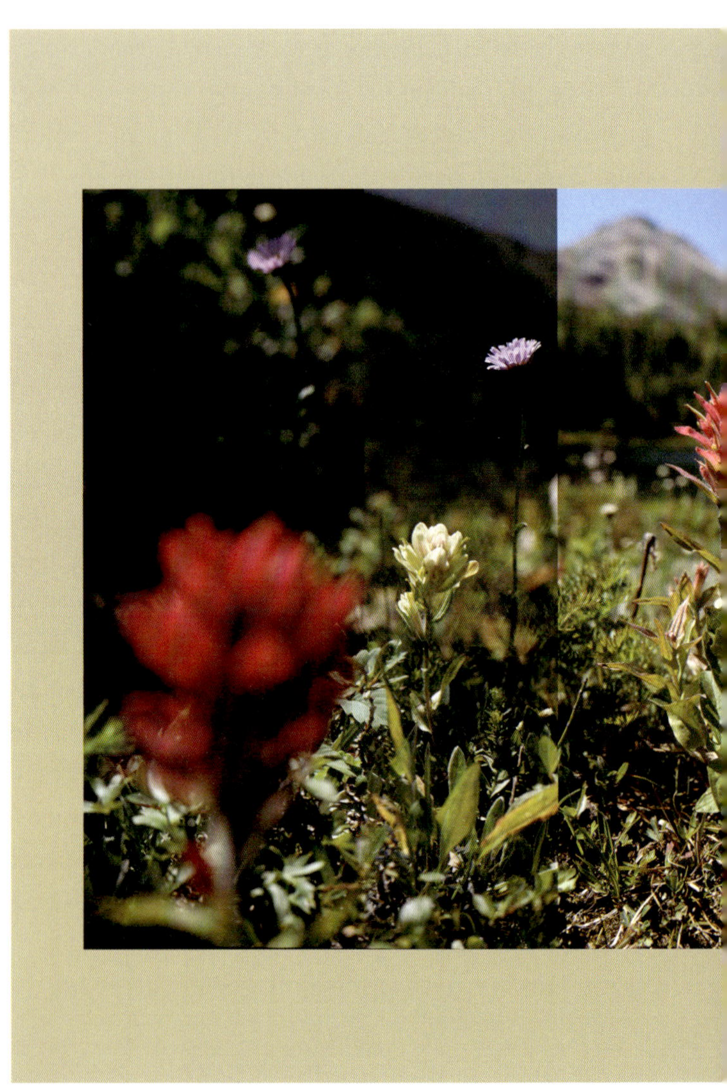

Indian Paintbrush at Sunshine Meadow

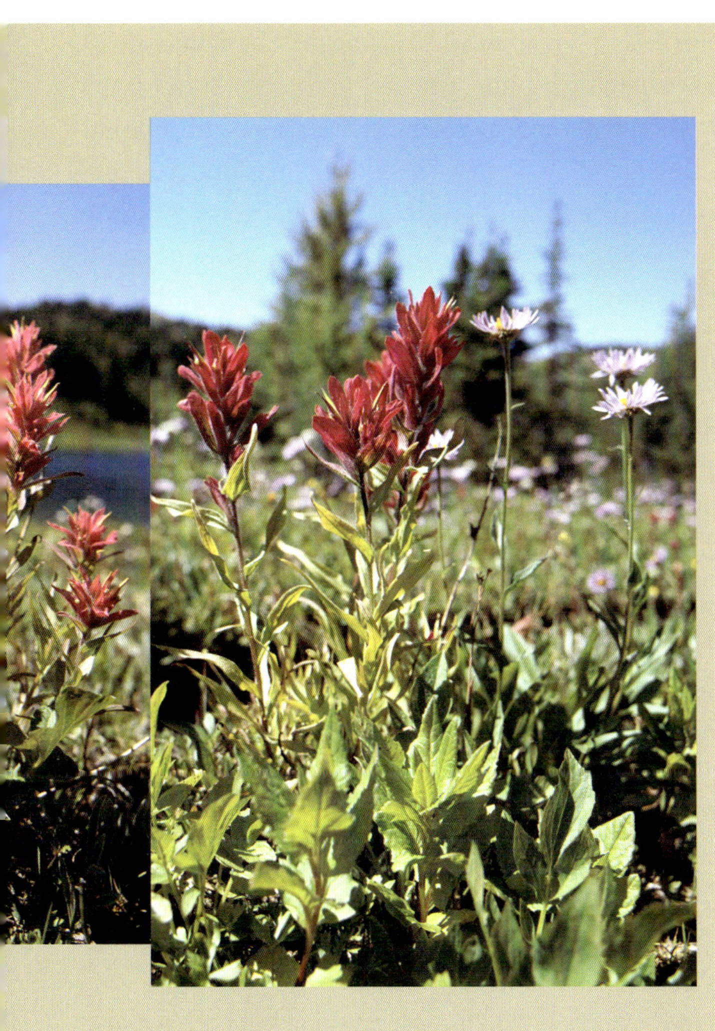

Brown's art, "flowers are like beings," Harmon remarks. "They have their own character, so the trick is to try and capture that somehow. Many people can record a beautiful picture of a flower but [in Brown's depictions] there is something more, in a poetic way, about them." Similarly, the poetic plays a role in Harmon's more mystical elaborations, such as the aforementioned *Western Wood Lily* and *Madonna Blue (Swamp Lantern)*. Created by layering images one over another, both works are part of series dedicated to the Roman goddess Flora, whose name became, in our western tradition, the collective designation for all vegetation.

Honoured in early May by the ancient Romans at the feast of Floralia, the goddess and what she symbolizes is celebrated in Harmon's portrayal of these two springtime beauties. Flora is supposed to have given the goddess Juno a miraculous flower with the help of which she became pregnant and gave birth to the god Mars. Could that flower have been the phallus-shaped *Lysichiton americanus* represented in *Madonna Blue*? With the presence of a woman with long, dark hair standing at the edge of a pool in the upper right of the photograph, there is ample opportunity to wonder.

Commonly known as western skunk cabbage because of its odour, this giant of the wetlands is one of the first

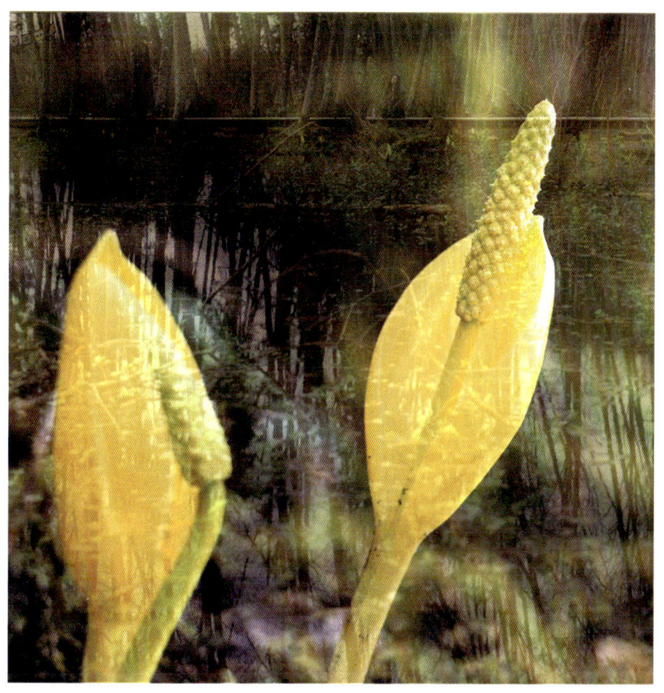

Madonna Blue (Yellow Skunk-cabbage)

flowers to poke its head above ground. While growing, it apparently produces enough heat to melt the snow around itself. No wonder that, at winter's end, its appearance captivates the eye of the photographer hungry for something fresh and new. William Copeland McCalla also shot this strange plant, with its metre-high yellow-green spike, or spathe (see page 65). He too uses the popular name that refers to the plant's unpopular smell, and today, in Mount Revelstoke National Park, along the Trans-Canada Highway, there is a self-guided tour of the nearby Skunk Cabbage Trail. For Carole Harmon's purposes, though, she prefers the plant's *other* common name, swamp lantern – an elegant moniker for a perennial that, in *Madonna Blue,* perhaps represents a beacon of light and hope.

Now a part-time inhabitant of Banff, Carole Harmon still feels she grew up in a park more than in a town with a world-famous name. "It's the wilderness thing," she explains. "It gave me a different experience of the world." In her photo-based art, it's an experience and now an engagement, not only visually contemporary for its own time but also enriched by the artistic legacy of those other hunters of flora and those held spellbound by the mountainscapes of her native home.

Notes

1. Lucia Tongiorgi Tomasi, "Nature Portrayed: Botanical Painting from Antiquity to the Contemporary Age," in *A New Flowering: 1000 Years of Botanical Art*, edited by Shirley Sherwood et al. (Oxford: Ashmolean Museum, 2005, published in conjunction with the exhibition of the same name at the museum May 2 to Sep. 11, 2005, curated by Shirley Sherwood): 11.
2. Annora Brown, *Old Man's Garden*, 2nd ed. (Sidney, BC: Gray's Publishing Ltd., 1970): 40.
3. Janice Sanford Beck, *No Ordinary Woman: The Story of Mary Schäffer Warren* (Calgary: Rocky Mountain Books, 2001): 152.
4. Ibid., 155.
5. E.J. Hart, ed., *A Hunter of Peace: Mary T.S. Schäffer's Old Indian Trails of the Canadian Rockies* (Banff: Whyte Foundation, 1980): 11, citing "Two Women in an Untrod Land," *New York Times*, Jul. 16, 1911. Full text of the latter [PDF image] available by searching the quote at nytimes.com (accessed Nov. 25, 2011).
6. Rudyard Kipling, *The Writings in Prose and Verse of Rudyard Kipling*, vol. 28, *Letters of Travel (1892–1913)* (New York: Charles Scribner's Sons, 1920): 220. Full text (unpaginated) available at archive.org, http://is.gd/gPD7LX (accessed Nov. 25, 2011).
7. Beck, *No Ordinary Woman: The Story of Mary Schäffer Warren*, 86.
8. Tomasi, "Nature Portrayed," 9.

9. Hart, *A Hunter of Peace*, 6.
10. Neil L. Jennings, *Uncommon Beauty: Wildflowers and Flowering Shrubs of Southern Alberta and Southeastern British Columbia* (Calgary: Rocky Mountain Books, 2006): 197.
11. US Bureau of Labor Statistics, "CPI Inflation Calculator," www.bls.gov/data/inflation_calculator.htm (accessed Nov. 25, 2011).
12. Mary Schäffer Warren, "Haunts of the Wild Flowers of the Canadian Rockies," *Canadian Alpine Journal* 3 (1911): 131. Full text available at archive.org, http://is.gd/ZIWZdP (accessed Nov. 25, 2011).
13. Interview with Henry James Vaux, Canmore, Alberta, Aug. 2009.
14. Cyndi Smith, *Off The Beaten Track: Women Adventurers and Mountaineers in Western Canada* (Jasper, Alberta: Coyote Books. 1989): 29.
15. Vaux interview, Aug. 2009.
16. Smith, *Off The Beaten Track*, 28.
17. Vaux interview, Aug. 2009.
18. Cavell, *Legacy in Ice*, 18.
19. Quotes by Mary Vaux Walcott are from her foreword in vol. 1 of *North American Wild Flowers* (Washington, DC: Smithsonian Institution, 1925).
20. Smith, *Off the Beaten Track,* 43–44.
21. Vaux interview, Aug. 2009.
22. Ellis L. Yochelson, *Smithsonian Institution Secretary, Charles Doolittle Walcott* (Kent, Ohio: Kent State University Press, 2001): 519.

23. US Bureau of Labor Statistics, "CPI Inflation Calculator," www.bls.gov/data/inflation_calculator.htm (accessed Nov. 25, 2011).
24. Smith, *Off the Beaten Track*, 15.
25. Terry Abraham, *Mountains So Sublime: Nineteenth-Century British Travellers and the Lure of the Rocky Mountain West* (Calgary: University of Calgary Press, 2006): 2.
26. Personal communication with descendants of the McCalla family in the form of a questionnaire to which the family replied by email Jun. 23, 2010. My thanks to Dennis McCalla, Donna Clandfield, Bob McCalla and Eric and Edie Stewart.
27. Toronto: Musson, 1920. The work is dedicated to Margaret McCalla.
28. McCalla family, *The W.C. McCalla Family*, edited by Pat Davidson, with production by Peggy McCalla (Halifax: Proper T Projects, 2006): 8.
29. Ibid., 10.
30. Roger Vick, "William McCalla, Naturalist," *Alberta History* 41, no. 3 (Summer 1993): 19–21.
31. McCalla, *Wild Flowers of Western Canada*, 59.
32. Ibid.
33. Ibid., 57.
34. Personal communication with McCalla family cited *ante* at p. 24.
35. Ibid.
36. Annora Brown, *Sketches from Life* (Edmonton: Hurtig Publishers Ltd., 1981): 8.

37. Annora Brown, *Old Man's Garden*, Sidney, BC: Gray's Publishing Ltd., 1970): 2–3.

38. George Melnyk, *The Literary History of Alberta*, vol. 2. (Edmonton: University of Alberta Press, 1998): 127.

39. Patricia A. Alderson, "Annora Brown: Forming a Regionalist Sensibility" (Master's thesis, Department of Art, University of Calgary, 2005): 58.

40. Ibid., 15.

41. Annora Brown, *Sketches from Life*, 74.

42. Ibid., 75.

43. Ibid.

44. Ibid., 76.

45. Ibid.

46. Ibid., 155.

47. Ibid., 94.

48. Ibid., 108.

49. Ibid., 105.

50. Ibid.

51. Ibid., 8.

52. Patricia A. Alderson, "Annora Brown: Forming a Regionalist Sensibility," 63.

53. Ibid., 37.

54. Ibid., 79.

55. *Sketches from Life*, 42.

56. *Old Man's Garden*, 187.

57. Ibid., 196–197 (all quotes in this paragraph).

58. Patricia A. Alderson, "Annora Brown: Forming a Regionalist Sensibility," 59.

59. Ibid., 5.

60. E-mail to author, Jan. 20, 2009.

61. Interview with the artist, Edmonton, Feb. 21, 2009.

62. Ibid.

63. Patricia Myers, "Capturing the Garden," *Legacy Magazine* (Fall 2002): 51.

64. Interview with the artist, Feb. 21, 2009.

65. Gillean Daffern, *Canmore & Kananaskis Country*, 2nd ed. (Calgary: Rocky Mountain Books, 2003): 75.

66. Ben Gadd, *Handbook of the Canadian Rockies*, 2nd ed. (Jasper, Alberta: Corax Press, 1995): 300.

67. Neil L. Jennings, *In Plain Sight: Exploring the Natural Wonders of Southern Alberta* (Calgary: Rocky Mountain Books, 2010): 135.

68. *Old Man's Garden*, 197.

69. John Allison Forbes. *Robert Sinclair: An Eight Year Survey* (Toronto: Aggregation Gallery 1976): unpaginated.

70. Robert Swain, *Pertaining to Space: An Exhibition of Work by Robert Sinclair* (Toronto: Art Gallery of Ontario, 1976): unpaginated.

71. Interview with the artist, Feb. 21, 2009.

72. "Alberta Wildflower Series" press release (Banff: Willock & Sax Gallery, Aug. 2, 2008).

73. Elizabeth Beauchamp, "Floral contemplation replaces prairie vision," *Edmonton Journal*, Apr. 15, 1989, F1.

74. Interview with the artist, Banff, Sep. 18, 2010. All subsequent quotes are from this conversation.

75. Loren Eiseley, "How Flowers Changed the World," in *The Immense Journey* (New York: Random House, 1957): 78.

76. Robert W. Sandford, *Ecology & Wonder in the Canadian Rocky Mountain Parks World Heritage Site* (Edmonton: Athabasca University Press, 2010): 71-72.

Sources and further reading

Abraham, Terry. *Mountains So Sublime: Nineteenth-Century British Travellers and the Lure of the* Rocky *Mountain West*. Calgary: University of Calgary Press, 2006.

Alderson, Patricia A. "Annora Brown: Forming a Regionalist Sensibility." Master's thesis, Department of Art, University of Calgary, 2005.

Beauchamp, Elizabeth. "Floral contemplation replaces prairie vision." *Edmonton Journal*, April 15, 1989, F1.

Beck, Janice Sanford. *No Ordinary Woman: The Story of Mary Schäffer Warren*, Calgary: Rocky Mountain Books, 2006.

Bown, Stephen R., and Nicky L. Brink. "Mountain Woman." *The Beaver: Canada's History Magazine* 87, no. 3 (June/July 2007): 42–46.

Brennan, Brian. *Alberta Originals: Stories of Albertans Who Made a Difference*. Calgary: Fifth House, 2001.

Brown, Annora. *Old Man's Garden*. 2nd ed. Sidney, BC: Gray's Publishing Ltd., 1970.

———. *Sketches from Life*. Foreword by Frank Lynch-Staunton. Edmonton: Hurtig Publishers Ltd., 1981.

Brown, Stewardson, with illustrations by Mrs. Charles Schäffer. *Alpine Flora of the Canadian Rocky Mountains*. New York: G.P. Putnam's Sons, 1907. Full text available at archive.org, http://is.gd/AtFkZR (accessed Nov. 25, 2011).

Cavell, Edward. *Legacy in Ice: The Vaux Family and the Canadian Alps*. Banff: The Whyte Foundation, 1983.

Cormack, R.G.H. *Wildflowers of Alberta*. Edmonton, Hurtig Publishers, 1977. First published 1967 by Alberta Dept. of Industry & Development.

Daffern, Gillean. *Canmore & Kananaskis Country: Short Walks for Inquiring Minds*. 2nd ed. Calgary: Rocky Mountain Books, 2003.

Eiseley, Loren. "How Flowers Changed the World." In *The Immense Journey*, 61–78. New York: Random House, 1957.

Forbes, John Allison. *Robert Sinclair: An Eight-year Survey*. Toronto: Aggregation Gallery 1976.

Gadd, Ben. *Handbook of the Canadian Rockies*. 2nd ed. Jasper, Alta.: Corax Press, 1995.

Hallworth, Beryl, and Monica Jackson. *Pioneer Naturalists of the Rocky Mountains and the Selkirks*. Calgary: Calgary Field Naturalists' Society, 1985.

Harmon, Byron. *Great Days in the Rockies: The Photographs of Byron Harmon, 1906–1934*. Edited by Carole Harmon and the Peter Whyte Foundation, with a biography by Bart Robinson and an appreciation by Jon Whyte. Banff: Altitude Publishing, 1984. First published 1978 by Oxford University Press.

Harmon, Don. *Columbia Icefield: A Solitude of Ice*. Photographs by Don Harmon, with text by Bart Robinson. Banff: Altitude Publishing, 1981.

Hart, E.J., ed. *A Hunter of Peace: Mary T.S. Schäffer's Old Indian Trails of the Canadian Rockies*. Banff: Whyte Foundation, 1980.

Jennings, Neil L. *In Plain Sight: Exploring the Natural Wonders of Southern Alberta*. Calgary: Rocky Mountain Books, 2010.

———. *Uncommon Beauty: Wildflowers and Flowering Shrubs of Southern Alberta and Southeastern British Columbia*. Calgary: Rocky Mountain Books, 2006.

Kershaw, Linda. *Alberta Wayside Wildflowers*. Edmonton: Lone Pine Publishing, 2003.

Kipling, Rudyard. *The Writings in Prose and Verse of Rudyard Kipling*. Vol. 28, *Letters of Travel (1892–1913)*. New York: Charles Scribner's Sons, 1920. Full text (unpaginated) available at archive.org, http://is.gd/gPD7LX (accessed Nov. 25, 2011).

Lang, Michale. *An Adventurous Woman Abroad: The Selected Lantern Slides of Mary T.S. Schäffer*. Calgary: Rocky Mountain Books, 2011.

McCalla Family. *The W.C. McCalla Family*. Edited by Pat Davidson with production by Peggy McCalla. Halifax: Proper T Projects (2006).

McCalla, William Copeland. *Wild Flowers of Western Canada*. Toronto: Musson, 1920.

Melnyk, George. *The Literary History of Alberta*. Vol. 2. Edmonton: University of Alberta Press, 1998.

Mitchell, W.O. *Who Has Seen the Wind?* Toronto: Macmillan of Canada, 1947.

Myers, Patricia. "Capturing the Garden." *Legacy Magazine* (Fall 2002).

Panzer, Mary. *Philadelphia Naturalistic Photography, 1865–1906*. New Haven, Conn.: Yale University Art Gallery, 1982, published in conjunction with the exhibition of the same name at the gallery February 10 to April 7, 1982.

Rickett, H.W. *Wildflowers of America: From Paintings by Mary Vaux Walcott*. New York: Crown Publishers Inc., 1978.

Sandford, Robert W. *Ecology & Wonder in the Canadian Rocky Mountain Parks World Heritage Site*. Edmonton: Athabasca University Press, 2010.

Sanford Beck, Janice. *No Ordinary Woman: The Story of Mary Schäffer Warren*. Calgary: Rocky Mountain Books, 2001 (3rd printing 2006).

Schäffer, Mary T.S. *Old Indian Trails of the Canadian Rockies.* Mountain Classics Collection 2. Calgary: Rocky Mountain Books, 2011. First published 1911 by G.P. Putnam's Sons, New York.

Schäffer Warren, Mary. "Haunts of the Wild Flowers of the Canadian Rockies." *Canadian Alpine Journal* 3 (1911): 131–135. Full text available at archive.org, http://is.gd/ZIWZdP (accessed Nov. 25, 2011).

Skidmore, Colleen, ed. *This Wild Spirit: Women in the Rocky Mountains of Canada*. Edmonton: University of Alberta Press, 2006.

Smith, Cyndi. *Off The Beaten Track: Women Adventurers and Mountaineers in Western Canada*. Jasper, Alta.: Coyote Books, 1989.

Swain, Robert. *Pertaining to Space: An Exhibition of Work by Robert Sinclair*. Toronto: Art Gallery of Ontario, 1976.

Tippett. Maria. *By a Lady: Celebrating Three Centuries of Art by Canadian Women*. Toronto: Penguin Group, 1992.

Tomasi, Lucia Tongiorgi. "Nature Portrayed: Botanical Painting from Antiquity to the Contemporary Age." In *A New Flowering: 1000 Years of Botanical Art*, edited by Shirley Sherwood et al. Oxford: Ashmolean Museum, 2005, published in conjunction with the exhibition of the same name at the museum May 2 to September 11, 2005, curated by Shirley Sherwood.

Vick, Roger. "William McCalla, Naturalist." *Alberta History* 41, no. 3 (Summer 1993): 19–21.

Walcott, Mary Vaux. *North American Wild Flowers.* Vol. 1. Washington, DC: Smithsonian Institution, 1925.

Wilkinson, Kathleen. *Wildflowers of Alberta: A Guide to Common Wildflowers and Other Herbaceous Plants*. Edmonton: University of Alberta Press, 1999.

Yochelson, Ellis L. *Smithsonian Institution Secretary, Charles Doolittle Walcott*. Kent, Ohio: Kent State University Press, 2001.

List of Artworks

page 20 Photographer unknown
Mary Schäffer Warren and Billy Warren, n.d.
Courtesy: Whyte Museum of the Canadian Rockies

page 23 Mary Schäffer Warren
Lady Slipper 1907
Cypripedium calceolus
watercolour
25 x 17 cm
Courtesy: Whyte Museum of the Canadian Rockies

page 29 Mary Schäffer Warren
Wild Roses n.d.
Rosa acicularis
watercolour
25 x 17 cm
Courtesy: Whyte Museum of the Canadian Rockies

page 31 Mary Schäffer Warren
Rubus parviflorus (Thimbleberry) 1907
Rubus parviflorus
watercolour
25 x 17 cm
Courtesy: Whyte Museum of the Canadian Rockies

page 32 Mary Schäffer Warren
Crocus (Pasque flower) 1907
Pulsatilla patens
watercolour
25 x 17 cm
Courtesy: Whyte Museum of the Canadian Rockies

page 34 Mary Schäffer Warren
Sambucus racemosa (Red Elderberry) n.d.
Sambucus racemosa var. *arborescens*
watercolour
25 x 17 cm
Courtesy: Whyte Museum of the Canadian Rockies

page 37 Mary Schäffer Warren
Campanula rotundifolia (Harebell) n.d.
Campanula rotundifolia
watercolour
25 x 17 cm
Courtesy: Whyte Museum of the Canadian Rockies

page 38 Photographer unknown
Mary Vaux Walcott collecting wild flowers in Canada, 1920s
Courtesy: Smithsonian Institution Archives

page 42 Mary Vaux Walcott
Rocky Mountain Cassiope (Western Mountain Heather) n.d.
Cassiope mertensiana
watercolour
20.3 x 25.4 cm
Archives & Library, Whyte Museum of the Canadian Rockies

page 46 Mary Vaux Walcott
Lake Louise Arnica n.d.
Arnica louiseana
watercolour
20.3 x 25.4 cm
Archives & Library, Whyte Museum of the Canadian Rockies

page 48 Mary Vaux Walcott
Alberta Paintbrush (Indian Paintbrush) n.d.
Castilleja miniata
watercolour
20.3 x 25.4 cm
Archives & Library, Whyte Museum of the Canadian Rockies

page 50 Mary Vaux Walcott
Silverberry (Wolf Willow) n.d.
Elaeagnus commutata
watercolour
20.3 x 25.4 cm
Archives & Library, Whyte Museum of the Canadian Rockies

page 53 Mary Vaux Walcott
Western Larch n.d.
Larix occidentalis
watercolour
20.3 x 25.4 cm
Archives & Library, Whyte Museum of the Canadian Rockies

page 56 Mary Vaux Walcott
Alpine Forget-me-not n.d.
Myosotis alpestris
watercolour
20.3 x 25.4 cm
Archives & Library, Whyte Museum of the Canadian Rockies

page 58 Photographer unknown
William Copeland McCalla, 1938.
Courtesy: Donna L. Clandfield

page 62 William Copeland McCalla
Movements of Floral Parts: *Parnassia fimbriata*: Showing how stamens expand one by one
circa 1926–1938
Parnassia fimbriata
from hand-painted slide (8.26 x 10.16 cm)
Provincial Archives of Alberta

page 65 William Copeland McCalla
Lysichiton camtschatcense – Western Skunk Cabbage
circa 1926–1938
Lysichiton americanus
from hand-painted slide (8.26 x 10.16 cm)
Provincial Archives of Alberta

page 71 William Copeland McCalla
Dandelion heads in fruit, open and closed
circa 1926–1938
Taraxacum officinale
from hand-painted slide (8.26 x 10.16 cm)
Provincial Archives of Alberta

page 72 William Copeland McCalla
Monotropa hypopitys – Many Flowered Indian Pipe
circa 1926–1938
Monotropa hypopitys
from hand-painted slide (8.26 x 10.16 cm)
Provincial Archives of Alberta

page 73 William Copeland McCalla
Shepherdia argentea – Buffalo Berry
circa 1926–1938
Shepherdia argentea
from hand-painted slide (8.26 x 10.16 cm)
Provincial Archives of Alberta

page 75 William Copeland McCalla
Bear Grass (Glacier Park)
circa 1926–1938
Xerophyllum tenax
from hand-painted slide (8.26 x 10.16 cm)
Provincial Archives of Alberta

page 78 Photographer unknown
Annora Brown, 1945.
Courtesy: Patricia Alderson

page 89 Annora Brown
Purple Flowers (Blue Clematis) n.d.
Clematis columbiana
watercolour
25.5 x 35.5 cm
Courtesy: Arctos & Bird

page 92 Annora Brown
Bluebells (Harebell) n.d.
Campanula rotundifolia
watercolour
13.5 x 8.6 cm
Courtesy: Alberta Foundation for the Arts

page 94 Annora Brown
Shooting Star n.d.
Dodecatheon radicatum
watercolour
27 x 35 cm
Courtesy: The Eleanor Luxton Historical Foundation

page 97 Annora Brown
Twin Flower & Canada Dogwood n.d.
Linnaea borealis & *Cornus canadensis*
watercolour
27.5 x 37.5 cm
Courtesy: The Eleanor Luxton Historical Foundation

page 98 Annora Brown
Coneflowers n.d.
Ratibida columnifera
watercolour
30 x 25 cm
Courtesy: Patricia Alderson

page 100 Annora Brown
Wild Rose n.d.
Rosa acicularis
watercolour
14.5 x 8.9 cm
Courtesy: Alberta Foundation for the Arts

page 100 Annora Brown
Rosehip n.d.
Rosa acicularis
watercolour
14.4 x 9 cm
Courtesy: Alberta Foundation for the Arts

page 102 Photographer unknown
Robert Sinclair, n.d.
Courtesy: Whyte Museum of the Canadian Rockies

page 104 Robert Sinclair, RCA
Sheltered Up (a.w.s.) Marsh Marigold, Edmonton 2004
Caltha palustris
watercolour/Arches paper
15 x 15 cm
Courtesy: Willock & Sax Gallery

page 106 Robert Sinclair, RCA
Youth Open (a.w.s.) Wood Lily, Jasper 2004
Lilium philadelphicum
watercolour/Arches paper
15 x 15 cm
Courtesy: Willock & Sax Gallery

page 108 Robert Sinclair, RCA
Shy Salute (a.w.s.) Yellow Lady's Slipper, Edmonton 2004
Cypripedium calceolus
watercolour/Arches paper
15 x 15 cm
Courtesy: Willock & Sax Gallery

page 111 Robert Sinclair, RCA
Double Shot (a.w.s.) Prairie White Wild Rose, Cypress Hills 2004
Rosa woodsii
watercolour/Arches paper
15 x 15 cm
Courtesy: Willock & Sax Gallery

page 117 Robert Sinclair, RCA
Passaged Dance (Mountain Memory) Fireweed, Willmore Wilderness 2006
Epilobium angustifolium
watercolour/Arches paper
28 x 38 cm
Courtesy: Willock & Sax Gallery

page 118 Robert Sinclair, RCA
Flower Rain (a.w.s.) Cowparsnip 2006
Heracleum lanatum
watercolour/Arches paper
28 x 38 cm
Courtesy: Willock & Sax Gallery

page 120 Photograph by Gary Sill
Carole Harmon, 2010
Courtesy: Carole Harmon

page 123 Carole Harmon
Wild Blue Flax n.d.
Linum lewisii
Photograph
36" x 36"
Courtesy: Carole Harmon

page 124 Carole Harmon
Old Man's Whiskers n.d.
Geum triflorum
Photograph
30" x 58"
Courtesy: Carole Harmon

page 126 Carole Harmon
Milk Vetch in Dinosaur Park n.d.
Astragalus canadensis
Photograph
22" x 50"
Courtesy: Carole Harmon

page 131 Carole Harmon
Western Wood Lily n.d.
Lilium philadelphicum
Photograph
36" x 36"
Courtesy: Carole Harmon

page 134 Carole Harmon
Indian Paintbrush at Sunshine Meadow n.d.
Castilleja miniata
Photograph
36" x 54"
Courtesy: Carole Harmon

page 137 Carole Harmon
Madonna Blue (Yellow Skunk-cabbage) n.d.
Lysichiton americanus
Photograph
24" x 24"
Courtesy: Carole Harmon

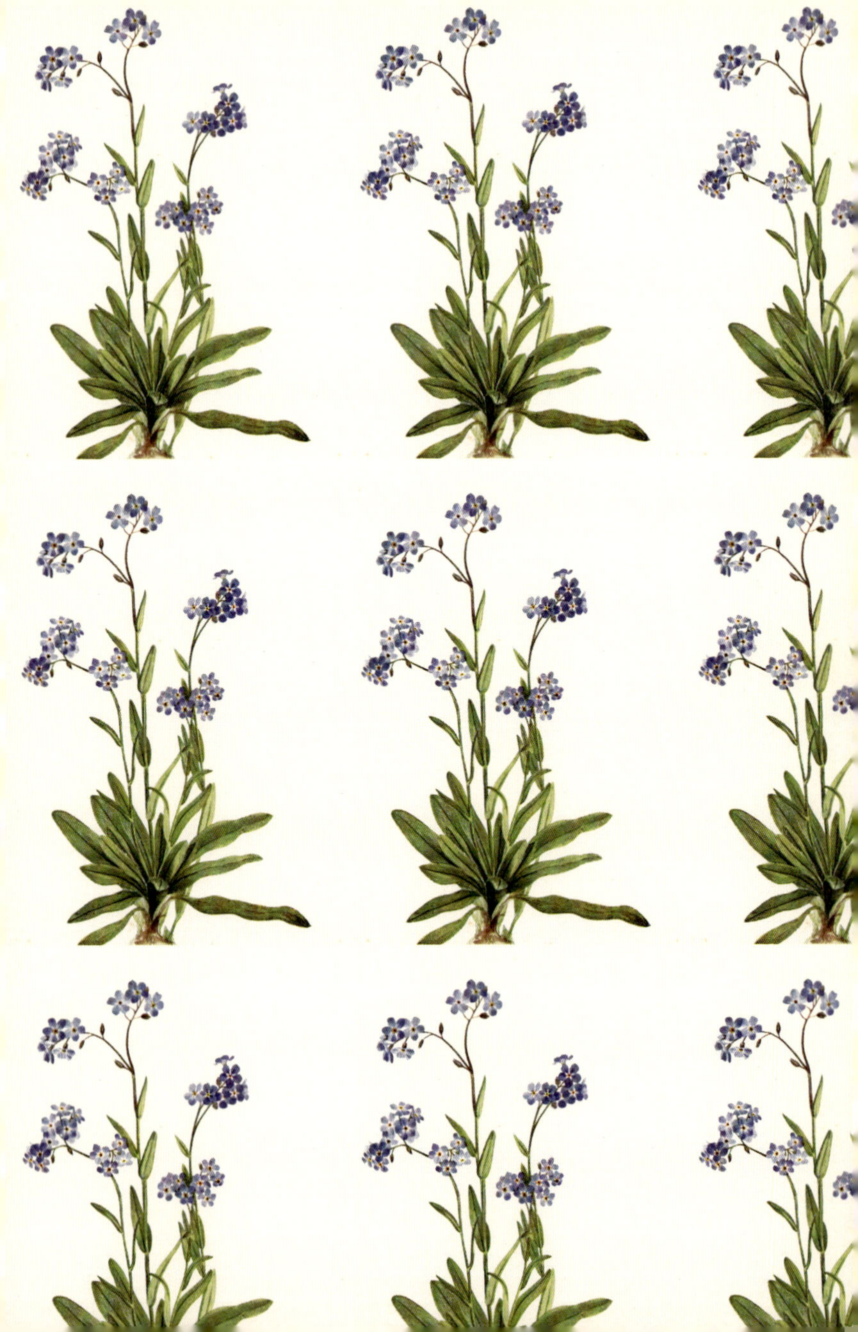